PRAISE FOR *A ROTTEN PERSON...*

"If you threw P.J. O'Rourke and Paul Theroux in a blender with some cheap rum and prune juice, you might get a cocktail as hilariously astringent as Gary Buslik's politically incorrect travelogue. This curmudgeon's tour of the islands should set tourism back a few years. Though...oddly...it makes me want to go there now. But that's probably the Chicago winter."

—Luis Alberto Urrea, author of *The Devil's Highway* and *The Hummingbird's Daughter*

"If I were an immigration officer in the Caribbean, I would never let this man enter my country!"

—Tom Miller, author of *Trading with the Enemy: A Yankee Travels through Castro's Cuba* and *The Panama Hat Trail*

"Fast-paced, quick-witted, and dangerously irreverent. Grumpiness has seldom been so much fun!"

—Elliott Hester, author of *Adventures of a Continental Drifter* and the bestselling *Plane Insanity*

"When Gary Buslik dies, study his brain. We have to prevent the same thing happening again."

—Daniel P. Luce, inmate counselor, Stateville Penitentiary, Joliet, Illinois

"I blame myself."

—Shirley Buslik, Gary's mother

Travelers' Tales Books

Country and Regional Guides
America, Antarctica, Australia, Brazil, Central America, China, Cuba,
France, Greece, India, Ireland, Italy, Japan, Mexico, Nepal, Spain,
Thailand, Tibet, Turkey; Alaska, American Southwest, Grand Canyon,
Hawai'i, Hong Kong, Middle East, Paris, Prague, Provence, San
Francisco, South Pacific, Tuscany

Women's Travel
100 Places Every Woman Should Go, The Best Women's Travel
Writing, A Woman's Asia, A Woman's Europe, Her Fork in the Road,
A Woman's Path, A Woman's Passion for Travel, A Woman's World,
Women in the Wild, A Mother's World, Safety and Security for
Women Who Travel, Gutsy Women, Gutsy Mamas,
A Woman's World Again

Body & Soul
Stories to Live By, The Spiritual Gifts of Travel, The Road Within, A
Mile in Her Boots, Love & Romance, Food, How to Eat Around the
World, The Adventure of Food, The Ultimate Journey, Pilgrimage

Special Interest
Not So Funny When It Happened,
The Gift of Rivers, How to Shit Around the World, Testosterone
Planet, Danger!, The Fearless Shopper, The Penny Pincher's
Passport to Luxury Travel, Make Your Travel Dollars Worth a Fortune,
The Gift of Birds, Family Travel, A Dog's World, There's No Toilet
Paper on the Road Less Traveled, The Gift of Travel, 365 Travel, The
Thong Also Rises, Adventures in Wine, The World is a Kitchen, Sand
in My Bra, Hyenas Laughed at Me and Now I Know Why, Whose
Panties Are These?, More Sand in My Bra

Travel Literature
A Sense of Place, The Best Travel Writing, Kite Strings of the
Southern Cross, The Sword of Heaven, Storm, Take Me With You,
Last Trout in Venice, The Way of the Wanderer, One Year Off, The Fire
Never Dies, The Royal Road to Romance, Unbeaten Tracks in Japan,
The Rivers Ran East, Coast to Coast, Trader Horn

a Rotten Person
TRAVELS THE
CARIBBEAN

GARY BUSLIK

Travelers' Tales
an imprint of Solas House, Inc.
Palo Alto

Travelers' Tales and Solas House are trademarks of Solas House, Inc., 853 Alma Street, Palo Alto, California 94301. www.travelerstales.com

Cover Design: Ian Shimkoviak, The Book Designers
Page Layout: Cynthia Lamb, using the fonts Bembo and CrustiEr

Library of Congress Cataloging-in-Publication Data

Buslik, Gary.
  A rotten person travels the Caribbean / Gary Buslik.
      p. cm.
  ISBN 1-932361-58-8 (pbk.)
  1. Caribbean Area—Description and travel. 2. Buslik, Gary—
Travel—Caribbean Area. I. Title.
  F2171.3.B87 2008
  972.9—dc22
                        2008003087

First Edition
Printed in the United States
10 9 8 7 6 5 4 3 2 1

For my friends.
This is what I was doing while you were making a living.

This is a work of nonfiction but some names and locations have been changed to protect the innocent, and in some cases, the guilty. Any resemblance to real persons of characters presented in a bad light is purely coincidental.

Table of Contents

The Time I Accidentally Urinated On Idi Amin

WE WERE IN MUSTIQUE, AN EASTERN CARIBBEAN "hideaway" island, and our taxi driver had just given us a drive-by of Mick Jagger's estate, Princess Margaret's winter mansion, and the vacation homes of two or three movie stars whose names didn't ring a bell, probably because I have not seen a movie since *The Exorcist*, which scared me so much that for a month I would not get up in the middle of the night to go to the bathroom, certain that Satan was waiting for me behind the shower curtain. It was not easy holding it in all night, but it wasn't the impossibility it would be now, my prostate currently being the size and consistency of a matzo ball. Not just any matzo ball, but one made by my cousin Linda, whose matzo balls are roughly the dimensions of the first atomic bomb. If President Truman had dropped one of Linda's matzo balls on Hiroshima, the Japanese would have surrendered in five minutes, and we would not have had to destroy Nagasaki three days later. I will get back to my prostate in a minute, which I promise has to do with Idi Amin.

I saw *The Exorcist* in a theater in an African-American neighborhood. Chicago is a city where ethnic enclaves are clearly marked by expensive, taxpayer-funded signs that arc over main streets. So it wasn't like I wandered into the neighborhood accidentally, got caught after the sun went down, and decided, what the heck, may as well see a movie about Satan. No, I went to that theater deliberately, because I happened to be dating Marceline, a black beauty from a wealthy Chicago Gold Coast family, and wanting to show her I was open-minded and adventurous and would therefore work well in her father's business empire, I picked a theater on the South Side.

Traditionally, film is a two-dimensional, nonparticipatory medium that limits its audience to sitting passively in a darkened theater while entering a troubled world of pretend characters, secure in the knowledge that when the lights come back on, the real, safe world will comfortingly reemerge. That pretty much describes your typical white-audience film experience.

But watching a horror film with a black audience is a different experience altogether, in which, Zen-like, the viewers *become* the movie, apparently believing not only that the events are actually happening to them personally and in real time but also that, corollarily, they can control the outcome. It's not a bad philosophy, actually. I've always thought it more sensible than the zombic passivity we associate with Caucasian moviegoing—not unlike the difference between a staid Presbyterian church service and a rip-roaring Baptist get-down. Don't just sit there stupidly, tempting the devil into thinking you're there for the taking. *Make some noise! Let that muthafucka know you ain't going down without a brawl!*

So, for example, in the scene where Father Damien haltingly approaches the upstairs bedroom in which Satan, in the body of Linda Blair, lies bound to the bedposts, my South Side audience, screeching "*Don't go in there! Don't open that door!! You crazy, man?! Don't open that door!!!*" jumped up, waved their arms at the screen, shrieked for their mothers, and fainted in the aisles—and getting up to buy popcorn was reminiscent of crossing the Gettysburg battlefield after Pickett's Charge. Except for the color, of course.

So you see that in that particular milieu, film was no longer a two-dimensional medium but one of at least eleven dimensions, including the Bizarro World, *The Twilight Zone*, the hotel in *The Shining*, *Nightmare on Elm Street* parts 1-4, and marriage. I will get back to that demented universe in a moment, and I still promise it involves Idi Amin. In the meantime, if Marceline happens to be reading this, I forgive you, and if you'll lift the restraining order, I'd still consider a position with Daddy's firm.

Our first day on Mustique, Annie, the woman I did marry and whose father was financially useless, was feeling giddy, thrilled to get away from her grueling Chicago routine of dog-earing catalog pages and having to repeatedly type our Visa number into her computer. Her mood changed the moment we walked off the plane, and the redolent tropical air burled up her elated nose. I had not even checked in to our guesthouse when she was hovering over her first poolside piña colada.

I returned from reception and handed her our room key. "Nice digs," I said. "What the hell is that?"

She followed my glance to a big, slobbering hog reclining two chaises over.

"A pig."

"He probably should put on some sun block."

"Isn't this the quaintest place? Pigs running free!" She pointed her orange slice at some shrubs. "Have you ever seen such red hibiscus? Such yellow bougainvillea? And a girl brings around a plate of fresh mango, and"—she inhaled—"doesn't it just smell like heaven?"

While she was going off on her Pollyanna riff, I couldn't take my eyes off the hog. I always try to see the bad side of everything, and the porker gave me the shivers. I knew something about voodoo, how the god Baron Samedi dresses up like a swine and visits people about to encounter grave misfortune. Annie mistook that malevolent porcine snorf for quaintness. But this is the woman who sees affection in the smiles of plumbers about to charge us $9,000 for recycled toilet seat bumpers. Of course, that would be my fault.

"They have diseases, don't they?" I asked.

"No more than we do."

"He wasn't in the pool, was he?"

"What if he was?"

"I was looking forward to a dip, is all."

"So take a dip. What do you want from me?"

"It hardly seems kosher."

"You know what?" she said testily. "Why don't you take a vacation in Haiti?"

So I knew it was time to find something cheery to talk about. Waving the daily activities sheet, I said, "Check this out. They're showing *The Exorcist* in the great house after dinner."

The waitress came over. I ordered a Diet Coke with lemon, and Annie ordered another piña colada. "Better go easy," I told her.

She scowled. "Why? Because it costs more than a nickel?"

So already I knew Baron Samedi was on the job. "Does this have anything to do with the fact that I tipped the taxi driver with Canadian money?"

"It has to do with the fact that you can't stand having a good time."

"I'm having a good time. They're showing *The Exorcist* in the great house. All week."

"For free, I suppose."

"What did I do wrong?"

"Diet Coke, that's what. Whoopee."

"With *lemon*."

"Can't you relax for once?"

"I don't need the calories, that's all."

"So now I'm fat."

"Did they make your drink extra strong or something?"

She sighed. "Here we are in paradise, and you want to stay around and watch a damn movie."

"With black people. Trust me, it's special."

"Live a little. It won't kill you."

"You want me to drink liquor?"

"Yes, I do. I want you to sip rum and go criminally insane and never be able to write again and stagger into the surf and get eaten alive by eels. That's what you're worried about, isn't it? That and losing all your teeth while you still have some dental floss left?"

"You know the deal with my prostate. Alcohol goes right through me. One cocktail, and it's up and down the rest of the night."

"I know, I know. And booze gives you gas, and you're terrified you might fart in front of me."

I raised my finger. "I'll be right back."

"You can't live your life afraid!" she called after me. "There's a pig lounging at the pool! Enjoy the moment!"

I went back to reception, chatted for a few minutes with the manager, and rejoined Annie in the sun.

"Scratch the movie. We're going dancing."

"Dancing?"

"At Basil's. World-famous nightclub."

"You're a horrible dancer. I wouldn't even call it dancing. It's like some weird quadriplegic thing. You hate music. Do you have any idea how sick it is to hate music?"

Not as sick as putting ketchup on hot dogs, I thought. But I kept my mouth shut. "True enough," I offered instead. "O.K., celebrity watching, then. They come to Basil's from all over the world. They tie up their yachts next door. Fly in on private jets."

"You hate celebrities."

"I thought you might like to get a little wild, that's all. First night in paradise? And then, who knows, afterward we come back to the room and—"

She got up and collected her towels. "You called me fat."

"Where are you going?"

"To the gift shop to max out our credit card."

So it was a pretty good bet it was going to be a long, lonely night.

My wife and I pretty much have nothing in common. She loves nature; I hate nature. Dark meat; white meat. Pepsi; Coke. Raisinets; Goobers. She has one cocktail every evening and likes to dance. That in itself should have been the red flag. The happy-hour habit she inherited from her parents, who also had a drink every night and lived well into their eighties but were blithering idiots the last couple of decades. The dancing, I don't know. To the best of my knowledge her parents didn't dance, and if they had, they would have careened off into different counties.

So when, at the hotel pool, I had stupidly blurted, "Better go easy," it probably hit too close to home DNA-wise, and the instant it came out I knew I was about to spend the next six nights in sexual solitary confinement.

Here is a secret for all you newlyweds: Drinking may make you puke, and dancing may make you dizzy, but blurting will destroy you with the blinding finality of cousin Linda's matzo ball on Hiroshima. Don't do it.

Basil's is a thatched beachside restaurant and nightclub built on pylons, hovering over Caribbean surf. From a distance it resembles a giant tarantula, squatting over its prey and sucking out its juices to the beat of reggae music. *Thump-thump-thump. Thump-thump-thump.* On Friday jump-up night you can hear the steel drums across Mustique and maybe on nearby Bequia and probably in Eastern Europe.

Apparently still miffed, Annie refused to take my hand as we crossed the planked boardwalk, waves frothing beneath us. I had to trick her into coming, telling her that Mick Jagger himself was on island and likely to show up. She was still not convinced that I wouldn't rather have been in the great house watching *The Exorcist*—right again—but reluctantly agreed, provided I would ask her to dance repeatedly so she could turn me down repeatedly, and provided that if I ordered a Diet Coke she could stab me in the neck with her fork. "No problemo," I assured her. "Now let's go have a good time."

The waitress looked us over, wondering, I guess, if we were famous. She put us in the middle of the room, the only table without a view of the water. When my eyes adjusted to the dimness, I glanced around for celebrities but saw none. I wasn't sure I would recognize any anyhow, so I sneaked a peek at Annie as she panned the room. Well, it was early, and maybe someone famous would still arrive, maybe even someone I recognized. Larry, Moe, and Curly were all dead, but if Linda Blair happened to walk in, *bingo*.

I tugged my dewlap. "So, would you like to dance?"

"Oh, no thank you."

In an hour the place was mobbed, and my Eustachian tubes calcified, or ossified, or whatever they do when parked next to six bombastic steel drum musicians auditioning for a record contract with executives listening from Los Angeles without benefit of a telephone. I was not alive when they built the Panama Canal, but my tympanic membranes could imagine what the isthmus must have felt like when that huge, hardened-steel, saw-toothed gnawing wheel ground its way from one ocean to the other.

Unlike unionized American musicians, West Indian bands do not take breaks. Caucasians are spoiled and weak, but blacks are robust and indefatigable. That is why eighteenth-century white men enslaved tribal Africans instead of union musicians. White slaves would immediately have called for collective bargaining, taken frequent coffee breaks, come down with carpal tunnel syndrome, insisted on cradle-to-grave health care and enormous pensions, and would have gone on strike anyhow, just for yuks. For a modern example: General Motors.

Annie was snapping her fingers, and her shoulders were dipping and gyrating. "Great music, don't you think?!" she shouted. "Good to dance to!"

"How about it?!" I shouted back, nodding at the dance floor.

"Oh, no thank you!"

I was pretty depressed knowing there wasn't going to be any nooky in my immediate future and that *The Exorcist* was probably half over. I glanced at my life partner licking her straw, and my ear canals felt like those rubber bands on toy propeller airplanes you wind up 400 times just so they can fly two feet before crashing into your face. I thought that the only thing that could get me the hell out of there would be a fatal heart attack—to either one of us, I didn't care—or, say, an international mass murderer waddling in and clearing the place out.

Well, guess what?

It happened while I was outside smoking a cigar. I promised Annie I wouldn't be gone long, so she needn't have worried about the band leaving before we had a chance to dance.

"Take your time!"

Fifteen minutes later, I tucked what was left of my cigar in its metal tube—waste not, want not—came back in and, not caring about other people, didn't notice right away that the crowd had become muted and brow-puckered. The band played as spiritedly as before, but now only one couple was on the dance floor, everyone else being huddled at their tables and looking as if they had just seen a cannibal or something. It didn't register at the time because, my prostate having plumped, the only thing on my mind was the men's room.

"Wait!" Annie yelped, grabbing for my wrist.

"We'll do the next song!" I promised and headed in.

There were two urinals. One was being used by a large black fellow shaped roughly like Mr. Peanut on cortisone but without the top hat. I was in the middle of attending to business, when I happened to glance in his direction, then glanced quickly away so he wouldn't think I was trying to cop a look at his you-know-what, did a double take, and realized that—whoa!—this was the brutal former Ugandan dictator who enjoyed dining on his enemies' entrails. So I did a triple take, this time swiveling my pelvis and appurtenances thereof, and before I could reverse direction—you can't stop a battleship on a dime—peed on the man.

It wasn't a waterfall, mind you, and mostly it wound up on his shoes, the problem being, he was wearing sandals. Big sandals, probably size 200, extra wide. I wear a 7 1/2 D. His toes glistened like tongues that have been cut out of the mouths of people who did not vote for him and thrown backward over his shoulder into Lake Victoria for good luck.

To understand why, on the one hand, I stood terrified of being beaten to death by a madman with a possible taste for Jewish food, but, on the other, as I abashedly tucked myself back into my shorts, I felt a tiny thrill at having just whizzed on the man who had butchered thousands of his countrymen, you need to know something about me.

I was born poor and without much prospect of success. My family got evicted a lot, and when we did live in actual apartments, they tended to be above bars. For my first seventeen years I wore only hand-me-downs from my cousin Sherwin, whom I despised. Sherwin liked to beat dogs within an inch of their lives and pull the abdomens off lightning bugs and grew up to be a gangster. To give you a good idea of the kind of guidance I had as a child, my father used to say, "Why can't you be more like Sherwin?"

Sherwin took a great deal of pride in his father being a slumlord, and maybe that's what my father had in mind when he told me to be more like my cousin. To Dad, a first-generation American, owning a skid-row flophouse was the epitome of success, and I suppose in his own demented way he wanted to inculcate me with good capitalist values, even though he could never seem to get his own ass out of bed before noon. And so I was expected to wear my cousin's discarded pants, shirts, shoes, socks, and underwear with gratitude. Sherwin knew I hated him and always gave me his old clothes dirty, adding skid marks—some in appropriate places, some not—for laughs.

At the time of my urinal encounter with Idi Amin, cousin Sherwin was selling used cars on the East Coast and still trying to figure out how in adding numbers you carried a digit from one column to another. When we were kids this process mystified him, but now he had apparently figured out a way to make a pretty good living at being mystified—when he didn't get caught. The Virginia Department of Commerce did call him in a couple of times, but apparently in the Washington D.C. region moral turpitude is not an impediment to staying in business.

So that having peed on Idi Amin, along with abject terror, I felt a kind of pride. My first thought was of Sherwin slogging through dirty snow on his funky used-car lot to screw some poor schlemiel out of dealer prep charges and processing fees. I thought of his baggy jeans I was forced to roll up seven or eight times and the stink of his underpants and the wads of newspaper I stuffed into his shoes to stop them from flapping. But now, thirty years later, here I was on a beautiful Caribbean island, in a world-famous night-club, with a gorgeous wife *praying* for me to ask her to dance, standing next to a former tyrant-for-life and current international pariah. Would I have rather peed on Mick Jagger's foot? Yes. Princess Margaret's? Of course. But for a kid whose parents couldn't afford to buy him a tricycle until he was halfway through high school, whizzing on Idi Amin wasn't nothing. It was something.

So I offered him a cigar.

My legs were wriggly, and I plopped myself next to Annie just before they gave out. Possibly sensing some-thing, she took my hand. The musicians were still beating the shit out of their oil drums, and I couldn't help think-ing that's what Idi Amin was going to do to my head as soon as he realized the cigar was already half-smoked.

"Did you see—"

"I urinated on him."

"Good God."

"It was the piña coladas. I tried to tell you."

"Why isn't he in prison?"

"Probably has something to do with the French."

"Maybe we'd better go."

I flagged down the check and forked over my credit card. But before the waitress came back with the receipt, out of the men's room waddled the mad cannibal, right over to our table—smoking my cigar stub. He asked Annie to dance.

"Oh, no thank—"

"Yes, thank you," I piped, elbowing her to her feet. "She'll be glad to dance. She loves dancing. Have fun, you two."

"Well," she stammered, "maybe…just one. My feet sort of hurt."

I hooked Idi a thumbs-up. Off they went, and I looked around frantically for the waitress with my receipt.

You're wondering if Amin was a good dancer, and the answer is, I don't know. You can tell with a jitterbug or even the twist, but calypso dancing is as befuddling to me as honest arithmetic is to cousin Sherwin. Idi certainly was trying hard, gyrating like a, well, madman, my cigar garroted between his fingers as he flailed around the dance floor, which he and Annie had all to themselves, the old kleptocrat—Idi, not Annie—using every square inch to strut his stuff. His movements were spastic and exaggerated, but he was an eater of human flesh, not Baryshnikov, so you work with what you have. I sort of felt sorry for him, to tell you the truth, because apparently he had had a lot of bottled-up emotion that he was finally able to let out in a nongenocidal way. The band fed off his volcanic energy and pounded their steel with foam-at-the-mouth frenzy.

Annie, meanwhile, kept throwing me desperate glances. Suddenly dancing was no longer the litmus test of whether or not you were emotionally healthy. One part of me was getting a kick out of it, but then I thought if I rescued her maybe I'd have a shot later in bed.

The song ended, and, with obvious relief, she cantered to our table.

"We all paid?" she panted.

"Here she comes now with the receipt."

"Let's get out of here."

The waitress stuttered, "Seems to be a problem with the credit card. Maxed out, looks like."

I squiggled my eyebrows—in Annie's direction, if I'm not mistaken.

The band started playing again.

"Splendid!" Idi exclaimed, snatching her hand. "Then we have time for more dancing!" He turned to me. "You're right, she's a terrific dancer! What a pair!"

I wasn't sure what pair he meant, but I couldn't think about that now. I was too busy explaining the situation to the woman at the credit card company. I don't think she believed me.

At ten-thirty the next morning the phone rang. I fumbled with it but managed to get it to my ear. I answered, then handed it to Annie.

"Who is it?" she mumbled.

"Your new best friend."

She jolted up and gagged the mouthpiece. "Idi Amin is on this phone?!"

"I knew someday music would get you into trouble."

She tried to shove me the phone. "Well, hang up, for God's sake!"

But with last night's piña coladas still calling, bladder-wise, I refused the phone and went to the bathroom. When I came back, she had hung up, and she looked as if her face had been sucked on by the aforementioned giant tarantula.

"He wants to go dancing again tonight."

"Not with me, I assume."

"What are we going to do?"

"We?"

"You're the one who peed on him."

I didn't say anything about the cigar. "What did you tell him?"

"The only thing I could think of. That we're hanging around to see *The Exorcist.*"

I brightened. "Really?"

"God, I hate you."

Contrary to appearances, though, things weren't going all that smoothly. I didn't tell her I had straightened out the credit card problem, so she wouldn't bolt off shopping again, and instead we sat at the pool all day, she reading Neiman Marcus catalogs, me blistering. Although I can't prove it without expensive lab testing, I swear she surreptitiously substituted my SPF 40 with Jell-O pudding. To further punish me, she ordered all the courses at dinner and ate almost nothing, which she knows drives me insane. At least I could console myself knowing that soon we'd be hearing the devil say dirty words to a priest. So it was back and forth like that, to see who could emotionally torture the other without actually admitting it—which had worked for twenty years, so why stop now?

Then, wouldn't you know it? At eight o'clock we're back in the room freshening up, all set to bound off to the great house, when she rubbed her temple and whimpered, "I've got such a headache. Why don't you go and see the movie by yourself? You don't mind, do you, hon?"

Treachery, thy name is woman! I should have seen it coming, I *should* have. *Twenty years!* But I had been so preoccupied with Satan and green vomit and Father Damien's dead mother groaning, "Why you do this to me Dimmy?" that I had let myself get sucker-punched.

"It won't be the same without you there getting grossed out," I muttered.

"Dig three Excedrins out of my suitcase, will you?"

"I mean, you're going to have a headache anyway. Why not just have it there?"

"I'm going into the bedroom now. Please don't wake me when you get back."

And away she went with her pills, leaving me defeated and miserable.

Resigned to my fate, I started to go out, when I heard her mewl behind me. She was standing in the bedroom doorway, still holding her Excedrins.

"What?"

"It's...*him*," she whispered. "At the *window*."

"Him who?"

"*Him* him."

I peeked over her shoulder. "I don't see anyone."

"He was *there*. Idi Amin. I'm not the psycho governess in *Turn of the Screw*."

"So in addition to being a mass murderer, he's also a Peeping Tom?"

"Get me the hell out of here!"

"I know. Let's go see a movie!"

And so it was that, on a starlit terrace, basted by a tropical breeze, rum punch in one hand, conch fritter in the other, my beautiful wife close by—although admittedly not close enough—and Linda Blair screaming obscenities on a large-screen TV next to a coruscating pool, I reached vacation nirvana. On the horizon, a cruise ship's lights twinkled fetchingly. But I was not to be fetched. I was content. And then who do you think stopped by, standing eerily in the shadows of a pool floodlight, looking around for you-know-who?

"Holy crap," Annie gulped, spotting him before he spotted her. "This isn't funny anymore."

He saw her, smiled, and waved.

"Don't panic," I said. "We've got plenty of witnesses."

"I'm not kidding. He's stalking me. Do something."

"Maybe he's just lonely, you know? I mean, everyone runs away from him."

"Good idea. Let's go."

I pulled her back. "He'll think you're just being coy."

Idi found a seat two rows behind us.

I whispered, "Only one thing to do. Get close to me. Real close. Let him know how much you love *me*."

She slid her chair close to mine and leaned against me like she meant it. I put my arm around her as I had when we were dating, and she nuzzled her blond head against my neck, and I hugged her and kissed her eyelid and her nose.

"I hate you," she whispered. "You understand that, right?"

"Better get closer."

It must have worked, because just as Father Dimmy was walking upstairs to Linda Blair's bedroom, I snuck a glance over Annie's shoulder and saw the former Ugandan dictator, no longer preoccupied with my wife, on his tiptoes, waving his fists and lunging at the TV, bellowing, "*Don't go in there! Don't open that door! Don't open that muthafuckin' door!*"

And then his eyes rolled up into the back of his head, and he hit the deck.

"You're in the clear," I told Annie.

"Good God. You think he's dead?"

"Trust me, he's fine. Check out this next scene. I promise, you won't want to go the bathroom for a month. And with any luck, neither will I."

"What's that smirk on your face?"

"I was just thinking of my cousin Sherwin."

"What the hell for?"

"He's been married four times, and I've only been married once. Happily, too."

She nuzzled closer, right up against my sunburn. I winced.

"What's the matter?" she said, pulling away.

"Nothing." I hugged her tighter. "Not a thing in the whole wide world."

My Military-Industrial Complex

THE CHECK-IN LINE AT JOSÉ MARTI INTERNATIONAL was for tourists what every other line in Cuba was for Cubans: long and languid and as listless as a python after eating an agouti on a sweltering afternoon. We had barely moved for almost two hours—sitting on our suitcases, reading, playing blackjack, muttering obscenities, occasionally standing to regain circulation and nudge our bags with our feet, playing Name That Tune on zippers and Hang the Butcher, with the Butcher sporting a beard, smoking a cigar, and wearing guerilla fatigues from the 1950s. But, like the Dow Industrial Average, in all that time we had gotten absolutely nowhere. One crummy check-in agent for a couple of hundred sunburned, bunion-throbbing, pissed-off Yanquis. Eventually the python began to bulge here and there, then break apart like on that New Hampshire Revolutionary flag, "Live Free or Die."

When I couldn't stand it anymore, I moseyed outside and found a kid—Raphael, nine years old—selling stale coconut fragments and gave him ten dollars to come inside and stand in line for me.

Let me explain something. In Cuba you can bribe anyone to do anything for a U.S. dollar. One night we went to the Museum of the Revolution, only to find it closed for "remodeling"—a term that is to Cuban economic reality what "international" is to Cuban airport. Well, fine. One dollar, and the security guard not only let us in and turned on the lights, he invited us to help ourselves to whatever mementos we might like, such as *Granma*, the boat on which Castro and a hundred of his men sailed from Mexico to launch their revolution. "Go on," he said, waving, "just take it."

If you got sick on hotel food and—the Cuban doctors being among the world's best—they diagnosed you with needing an entire upper-body transplant, and there were three thousand desperately ill Cubans on the upper-body waiting list, a buck would do the trick, and you'd be flying home with a spanking new thorax.

So in offering Raphael a sawbuck, I was not only giving him at least a thousand times more than necessary, I was also single-handedly reviving the Cuban gross domestic product. Unfortunately my wife didn't see it that way.

"What's the matter with you?" she hissed.

I explained about the Cuban economy.

"He's not standing in line for you. It's demeaning."

"Not as demeaning as constantly losing at Hang the Butcher. What the hell kind of a word is *sphygmomanometer*? You made that up."

"Not you. Demeaning for *him*, you twit."

"Now there's a word I can wrap my brain around."

"Send him back out there."

"He's selling chunks of old coconuts for a nickel. He'll be dead before he makes ten bucks."

"Then let him keep the ten dollars."

"It's not slavery," I pointed out. "He wants to work for it, and if you send him away, he'll think it's his fault.

Anyhow, what's so demeaning about standing in line?" I glanced around at our fellow travelers. "I'll bet they wish they'd thought of it first." She magnetized my molecules with her MRI glare—usually reserved for when George Bush says something idiotic, as if I, personally, had been responsible for the low oxygen level in his incubator. "Hey, we all work for someone."

"Not standing in line for spoiled Americans," she said. A fat Canadian with a ponytail in front of us shook his head—in disgust, if I wasn't mistaken. "Right on, sister," he muttered. Instead of a respectable, bourgeois suitcase with gimpy wheels, he nudged a backpack across the floor, the kind usually seen on the bony shoulders of pimply college undergraduates, not middle-aged men shaped like Shamu the whale. I knew he was an escapee from the Great White North because his passport was tucked into a strap on his backpack, as if he wanted to make damn well sure everyone knew he wasn't an American. You can pick out a Canadian passport from across a room, because its cover features a gold-embossed portrait of Queen Elizabeth eating a bacon sandwich. You can tell it's bacon by the curlicue tail sticking out of the bread.

I happen to like Canadians. Many years ago, my best friend, Steve, and I spent a week at a fly-in fishing camp in southern Ontario, on a system of lakes that, had Livingstone been fishing there, Stanley would not have found him in a bazillion years. The landscape was so unremittingly wet and featureless and bland, even Canadians considered it boring. It was like a Hamm's Beer sign had fallen into the sink, and the bartender accidentally left the cold faucet running overnight, and a storm came and blew the roof off the bar, and the bartender, who had fallen asleep drunk in the storeroom, drowned.

The lakes were so easy to get lost on that we were supposed to wear bright orange ponchos so the seaplane that had dropped us off would be able to find us in a week, and if we heard the plane but didn't see it, we were supposed to make a fire and, if necessary, burn all our clothing to attract attention. The problem being that we and all our belongings were so thoroughly soaked to the bone—if our belongings had had bones—that we could have doused ourselves with kerosene from our sleeping-bag warmers, had we not run out of kerosene four days earlier, and had our sleeping bags not fallen out of our capsized canoe, along with our food, tent, clothes, and ourselves, and they still would not have caught fire.

So we wound up fishing naked, which we found liberating and glorious and spiritual, until my accident with the lure. Then we had to call for an air ambulance, which cost $3,000 Canadian—$65 U.S.—but which at least supplied us with dry hospital gowns. They flew us to Winnipeg, where they surgically removed the lure and related minnow, and, after a massive dose of antibiotics, we saw an American movie with Canadian subtitles and went to a "massage" parlor where we could be with actual women, as opposed to walleye pikes dressed up like women. My "massage therapist" was a nifty brunette named Margo, who at the time reminded me of Jill St. John, but in retrospect more resembled Herbert Hoover. In any event, there I was lying on my back, "massage" towel draped over groin, and Margo dribbling warm "massage" oil into my navel while we engaged in preparatory idle chitchat. Then she asked me if I would like her to remove the towel, and I said sure, and when she saw what was underneath she screamed and asked what the hell was that. I told her it was

a fish-hook accident, but I don't think she believed me because she blew a whistle, and in ran a seven-foot-tall
Canadian with a hockey stick who threatened to slap-shot
me stupid if I did not scram and take my weird-looking
groin and my friend Steve with me. Or it may have been
the other way around.

So you might wonder why I like Canadians, and I will
tell you. A couple of years later the Blackhawks made it to
the Stanley Cup playoffs versus the Maple Leafs, and who
should turn out to be Toronto's star defenseman but Matt
Powell, Margo's seven-foot bouncer. I had just met Annie,
and I wanted to impress her on our first date, so I asked her
if she wanted to go to a playoff game, only to find that
tickets were pretty much impossible to get. So in despera-
tion I found out what bar the players hung out at, and I
took a chance and cornered Powell, and after very little
prodding he remembered that I was the fish-hook guy
whose arm he had threatened to tear off and beat me with,
and I bought him a Labatt beer, and we became new best
friends. He got me two front-row seats, and Annie thought
I was some kind of CEO or something, and I asked Powell
not to mention the Margo/lure incident in front of her,
and he never did. So we fell in love—me and Annie, not
me and the defenseman—and I thought she was a
Republican, so I married her.

And she was a Republican, too, until George W. Bush
got elected, at which time she became a communist, and
now she blames me personally for everything that comes
out of his mouth, including the hay. Somehow or other it
was *my* fault that we didn't find weapons of mass destruc-
tion in Iraq, that the levees failed in New Orleans, that
there was a volcanic eruption on Montserrat, and that Karl

Rove is the moral equivalent of smog. I am not allowed to watch Fox News while she is in the room or turn off any TV while set to that station, in case she should be the first to turn it on again. She is suddenly gung-ho for Hugo Chavez, reparations for blacks, and changing Chief Illiniwek's name to Chief Rotten Imperialist Pig. She now believes that *The Wall Street Journal* is an example of ideo-logical state apparatus; that maybe Thomas Jefferson wasn't such a great guy after all, considering he liked brown booty; that Fidel Castro is the second coming—assuming there had been a first, which she doubts; and that if George Bush had his way, Havana would be a Wal-Mart and the rest of Cuba a parking lot, as though the previous fifty years have been a figment of the Earth's imagination.

Reminding her that she had married me under possibly false pretenses fell on "audibly disadvantaged" ears, and she replied that if I wanted a divorce, fine and dandy, and if Bushy nominated one more evangelical Christian lunkhead to the Supreme Court, she had her divorce lawyer, Adolph Hitler Mendelbaum, ready to file, so I'd better pray for the justices' good health.

So, yes, I did like Canadians, but the muttering former hippie in front of us at José Marti "International" was a tad suspicious-seeming. For one thing, I had seldom seen a fat Canadian—they worked off their bacon by cleaning fish, I guess—and, for another thing, all the hippies I had ever known pretty much grew out of it in their twenties, when they traded in their roach clips for Audis and condos. The last time I had seen a ponytail on a man the age of this so-called Canadian was when they found that Green Beret alive in the Cambodian jungle, having survived there for thirty years and never knowing the war was over or that

Nixon had resigned and that America had matured to the point where we would teach creationism again in our public schools, and all he could eat was capybara poop until long and intense psychotherapy, during which he was gradually introduced to current movie prices and Ann Coulter.

So right off the bat I didn't like this corpulent, time-warped freakazoid, although based on what you already know about my wife, you probably thought she would have answered his clearly provocative, anti-American crack, "Right on, sister," with a raised-fist, black-power salute, like those putzes in the 1968 summer Olympics whose names no one even remembers, and that she would have given him a hippie handshake and trucked on down with him to the airport lounge, where they would have shared carrot juice and a toke, and they would have exchanged notes on how to blow up oil tankers.

You would think so, but you would be as wrong as a naked fisherman trying desperately to reel in a twelve-hook, Godzilla-brand lure that happened to be snagged on a sunken Canadian log. You cannot get more wrong.

Because here is an interesting thing about Annie. On the one hand, she will make a mad dash to Michael Moore's latest movie with the enthusiasm of one dog's nose up another dog's poo-poo, and she will return home spewing all manner of liberal claptrap to her emotionally needy, Bush-voting husband, who desperately wants a bit of nooky before bedtime. On the other hand, you can't make a sow's ear out of a silk purse, and I knew, just *knew*, that when it came down to it, if some foreign, Jefferson Airplane-loving weed-sucker dared to say peep against her country, she would de-spleen him with the efficiency of mongoose on snake.

And sure enough, recognizing that murderous, patriotic gleam in her eye, I both feared for the unsuspecting, pony-tailed lard bucket and, at the same time, braced myself for some yuks.

But, oddly, she pinged him with only a grazing look and said nothing. Instead, she turned to Raphael, folded his hand around my ten dollars, so he knew he could keep it, then pointed to the door and smiled maternally. "It's yours, honey. Go."

The kid looked at me, confused. "No change," he stuttered—probably a phrase he had learned phonetically.

Annie shook her head. "It's O.K., keep it."

Again, Raphael, frowning, glanced at me.

"No problemo," I said, loud and slow and showing my palms. "Keepo itto."

The Canadian clacked his tongue, flicked his ponytail, and rolled his pork-loving eyeballs.

Okey-dokey. Now he was really in for it. True, Annie had been perfectly willing to deal him a beginner's good hand. It had been his lucky day. He had pulled a pair of tens. But with that clacking he had pressed that luck, split his pair, and was about to get his head handed to him. He was about to be blonded.

I held my breath. This was it. Cobra, prepare to die.

She turned to me. "Fork over a twenty."

"Twenty what?"

Her eyes bulged. I whipped out my wallet and found a double sawbuck. She snapped it nice and loud—to irritate our Canadian enemy, I assumed. She handed the money to Raphael. "For you," she said. "You don't have to do anything. We have lots."

"We do?" I whispered, making a sound like a sneezing hamster.

She motioned for my wallet again.

"Um, don't you think this is the kind of thing we should discuss as a couple?"

She thrust out her palm and wriggled her fingers malevolently—again, undoubtedly for the benefit of our northern friend.

I handed her my wallet. She went right for the hidden pocket, where I kept my bail money. She handed Raphael two crisp hundreds. "For you to do whatever you want, sweet boy. Don't forget the rest of your family."

The Canadian said nothing. Evidently humiliated, demoralized, and defeated, he had returned to his crossword puzzle.

Annie took out two more hundreds from their leather lair, creased them lengthwise, and tucked them into the lad's pocket. "We're rich," she told him. "Wealthy Americans. Very spoiled." She turned to me. "Aren't we, dear?"

I cleared my throat. She handed me back my wallet with three dollars in it.

Did we show that Canadian, or what?! *These colors don't run!*

She patted Raphael's head. "Have a nice day."

The boy turned to me. I could see what was left of his lunch on his back teeth. Coconut.

"Yeah, have a nice day," I said. "Try real hard."

Annie tilted her head at me. I held up my hand. "O.K., I'm not saying another word."

"And you're going to keep me company in line and not get any more bright ideas?"

"You bet, and no way."

"Deal the cards, bright boy."

I did, and she drew twenty-one, and I busted. We sat on two suitcases and used the third as a table, and every now and then we'd inch along and continue playing, and after about an hour I dealt her a ten and a six and was waiting for her to indicate stay or hit, and when she didn't I glanced up and saw her looking around the hall, her mouth twisted weirdly, her eyebrows gnarled, and I followed her gaze and saw it too. I was the last one to see it, but that's the story of my life.

Raphael had put out the word, had rounded up a horde of his young *compañeros*, or whatever they're called, who were stampeding the waiting line with offers to stand in for passengers at a U.S. dollar each. In a few minutes Annie and I were pretty much the only non-Cubans still in line—the Canadian having been one of the first to fork over his buck, no doubt so he could rout up a pork sandwich.

It all worked out, though. I taught the urchins how to play blackjack, and when they lost their money, I explained about what we call in English the "learning curve" and made them repeat the phrase several times until you could hardly detect an accent, and after I won back my bail money, I let them play on credit, and when they continued to lose I was willing to let them work off their debt by walking on Annie's and my backs, which were killing us from having waited so long in line. At first she didn't like the idea, but when I pointed out that I was teaching them the evils of gambling, ancillary to the evils of capitalism, she, too, saw it as a life-lesson master stroke and flipped over on her tummy.

NASDAQ 5,000

We didn't get to the hotel until after dark. Everything was pretty much as it had been twenty years ago, except a little threadbare. We certainly could have afforded much better now, but Bajan Guest House had carved out a little place in Annie's heart. Even after all those years, the bartender, Horton, remembered us, making her very happy. He served us welcome punches, two cherries each.

"Here's to our second honeymoon," she whispered, wrapping her drink around mine.

I looked around the weary bar, at the sagging fishnet above the cash register, the broken starfish, the dusty bottles of rum. Maybe Bajan House was a buyout candidate. Maybe we could fix up the place, flip it, and make a quick couple of hundred thousand. But I kept my mouth shut. I just sipped my punch and returned my wife's kiss.

"What're you looking at?" she demanded.

"Nothing." I sucked my orange slice. "I'm just glad to be back."

"Your phone off?"

"You bet."

"Let's walk on the beach."

"Now?"

"What's wrong with now?" She nodded at the bar-tender. "Horton will let us take the glasses, if we promise to bring them back, won't you, Horton?"

"Of course, Missus."

With me puffing an outsized Cohiba, we strolled down Rockley Beach to the jetty, then back up Bay Street, Annie snapping her fingers to the rhythm of a steel-drum band playing at a nearby hotel, me thinking about NASDAQ. Yesterday it had closed over 5,000.

My cell phone rang, muffled in my pocket.

Annie cleaved me a glare.

"I thought it was off, I swear to God. Here, look, I'm shutting it off right now."

"Get to it."

I shoved my hand into my pocket.

"Well?" she snarled.

"What if it's an emergency? What if I take this one, then turn it off for the rest of the trip?"

She turned and kept walking. I let her get twenty feet ahead, then answered the call with a whisper.

"I have to turn off my phone," I told Neal, my broker. "Leave a message at the desk if we get filled on our WorldCom July 110s. Don't call the room. For God's sake, don't call the room."

I turned off the phone, put it back in my pocket, and raced to catch up with Annie.

"Off forever," I promised. "I thought I killed it at O'Hare." When I put my arm around her, she didn't protest. "I'll put out this stinky cigar, too."

"It's all right."

"It is?"

"But if I hear that phone again, I'll ask Horton to frappé

your nuts in a blender. That would make a heck of a welcome punch, don't you think?"

"No problemo."

As we walked hand in hand, the tension drained out of
her. "Everything's so different," she said, wistfully. "But
we're still the same, aren't we, honey? I don't mean Charles
Schwab-wise. I mean really the same inside."

Before I could reply, from the shadows between Café
Sol and Half Moon Apartments squirted a cadaverous beggar, his ribs protruding, his stomach concave.

"Want to buy me magic seed?" said the grungy, shirtless
Rasta, his hand extended. "You plant seed in yard, it grow
good luck."

I puffed harder on my Cohiba to cover up the stench of
the nearly toothless, shoeless, dreadlocked peddler. I
walked on, assuming Annie was right behind me. But
when I glanced back, I saw that she was actually talking to
the grunge. She took the seed and held it in her palm
while listening to his spiel.

I strode back, stepped between them, took a buck from
my wallet, handed it to the scruff, and took my wife's arm.

"Wait!" the beggar yelled, striding after us. "Where you
going wid me seed?"

I kept walking, but Annie pulled from my grip and again
stopped. I turned.

"Here's you fuckin' dollar, buoy!" the beggar shouted,
balling up the money and hurling it at me. "I don't want
you fuckin' dollar! Me want me seed back! Me seed worth
ten fuckin' dollar!"

I sized him up. He was wiry and hard, with features
sharp enough to gut fish. I had heard that West Indians
fight wildly—poking out eyes, ripping out hair, gnawing

off fingers. All I knew was good old-fashioned American punching. If the villain did rip out my eyes, I would never again be able to watch a ticker tape scroll on the bottom of CNBC.

Still, I had to protect my wife.

I turned around, and, just as she was opening her purse to give him ten bucks, I grabbed the seed from her fist and held it out for the pirate.

He cursed and muttered—I didn't understand a word—and spat like a snake. But, to my relief, he took back his seed. "Tief!" he bellowed, turning back into the shadows. "Damn tief! Tief me land! Tief me sugar! Tief me beach! Tief me coconut! Tief me rum!"

Annie's hand was halfway out with a ten-dollar bill. I nudged it back into her purse. I was proud of myself.

"Tief me pickney! Tief me coral! Tief me gal! Tief me fish!" His mud-crusted arms flailing, the beggar disappeared into the night.

"What are you doing?!" she snapped, tearing her hand away from mine.

I was startled. "What do you mean?"

"What do you mean, what do I mean?!" She crunched her purse closed and peered for the ruffian in the darkness. "What the hell is the matter with you?!"

"The matter with *me*?!"

"All he wanted was a few dollars."

"Ten dollars for a seed you can find everywhere?" My glance fell on a brown, boomerang-shaped pod in the gutter. "It was a common tamarind seed."

"Obviously, the seed isn't the point. Anyone but you would see that."

"You were actually going to give him ten dollars for that stupid story about good luck? We already have good luck."

"He wasn't referring to NASDAQ."

"He was taking advantage of tourists."

"We can afford it. He needs the money."

"To get more stoned?"

"Not *every* fee has to be discounted."

"No one in his right mind would give him ten bucks." She started to walk away. "Not everyone's Global B," she snorted, referring to my Charles Schwab account username.

"This is crazy," I reasoned, following her. "I offered him a buck, for Christ's sake. I didn't even want his stupid seed."

"He could have been a homicidal maniac for all you knew. He could have had a machete or something and whacked off my head."

"That's why I came back to help."

"You came back to see if you could get a better *deal*."

"He was wearing shorts. Where was he supposed to hide a machete?"

She swiveled. "Don't try to negotiate your way out of this one!"

"Out of what one?"

"The world according to Global B."

"I tried to give him a buck for a seed. He insulted us."

"Not us. *You*."

"He spit on me."

"I don't blame him in the least," she chuffed, striding away again. "We come here and throw their own seeds back in their faces."

"This is crazy."

"Global B."

"I *handed* it back to him."

She refused to look at me. "For ten lousy stinking dollars, you humiliated him in his own country."

"You just said he was a homicidal maniac. Now you're worried about embarrassing him?" I tried to step in front of her but sidestepped when she threatened to run me down. "Most wives would be grateful their husband came to their rescue."

She chortled.

Walking backward, I said, "What the hell do I care about ten bucks? My cigar cost twenty-five."

"Global B."

I fell behind, as she turned a corner. I felt wounded and perplexed. I wondered what the hell I did wrong.

I followed her back to Bajan House, and, with her safely inside, kept walking. I was plenty ticked. I relit, finished my cigar, and lit another with long, hard, ticked-off puffs. Fifty bucks worth of cigars, just like *that*.

But by the time, around midnight, I got back to the hotel, my anger had drained. The truth was, I had been looking forward all day to making love to Annie in the same room where we had spent our wedding night, amid the violin-chorus of tree frogs, lighted by the twinkle of cruise ships on the horizon or, if we were luckier still, by a cloudless moon. Love fueled by my unebbing adoration of her and by generous portions of Fire Mountain Heavenly Dark, the local rum we had discovered here twenty years ago.

She was just getting out of the shower, steam billowing out of the half-open bathroom door. I hoped the hot water had softened her spirits. But when she came out with her face globbed chartreuse, I realized she intended to go right to sleep.

She slipped under the sheet and rolled over on her side, her back to me, the coral-colored sheet draped over her perfect, teardrop-shaped body. Her waist was so thin I had always been able to wrap both hands around it and touch my fingertips. I ached with wanting to make love to her.

"I'm going to turn on the TV," I warned. "I'm not tired."

"It's no concern of mine."

"Won't it bother you?"

"It's none of my business."

"I might read. I'll have to turn the light up."

"Do what you want. Oh, by the way, there was a message for you at the front desk."

I acted surprised. "Really? What did it say?"

"It says, 'Screw yourself.'"

I found the message slip on the dresser and, without even taking a peek, crumpled it up for her benefit. I got into bed and leafed through the room copy of *Welcome Bonjour Willkommen Barbados*, rustling pages. When that didn't rouse her, I turned on the television and found WGN. "Good old Cubs," I muttered. "Yes, sir. Who doesn't love late-night sports?"

Nothing.

I looked up at the mosquito net, bundled above our four-poster like a storm cloud. I couldn't stand it anymore. I dropped the TV remote onto the magazine. "Why are you doing this?"

"Doing what?"

"You know what."

"Because it's been a long day, and I'm tired."

"I don't mean sleeping. You know what I mean. I mean acting like I'm Adolph Hitler."

"Have a nice second honeymoon, Global B."

"I didn't do anything wrong."

"Just tell me if you're going to jabber all night, so I can put in my earplugs."

"I've been trying to figure out how I could have been a better person there."

"You are what you are."

"Are you mad because we haven't taken a vacation together in three years?"

"Good night."

"I've been working my brains out."

"It shows."

"I offered him a dollar for a lousy tamarind seed!"

"You're starting to repeat yourself."

"All right. If that's the way you want it, I'm going for a walk."

"Be sure to turn off the Cubs."

"By myself. On our second honeymoon."

"Don't slam the door."

I threw on the same clothes I had worn on the plane—khaki Dockers and a long-sleeve shirt with Charles Schwab's logo embroidered over the pocket. I uncrinkled Neal's message—also for her benefit—started to leave, then stopped to turn on my cell phone, which came to life with a one-octave rendition of "God Bless America."

"Oh, good," I said, crackling the message slip again. "Filled at five and a half."

"Global B," she mumbled.

I didn't slam the door, but I sure as hell hadn't turned off the Cubs.

Downstairs, the lobby was dim and deathly quiet. The night clerk was gone somewhere, the bar was closed, the ceiling fans were still. A palm frond floated motionless in the coruscating pool, casting a prehistoric shadow. Three terra cotta steps led to the beach. Except for soundless lapping, the sea slept, flat as a mattress.

I walked the other way, onto Bay Street. That, too, was quiet, though glowing ghostily in neon. The silence was broken by laughter. Down the block a young tourist couple walked arm in arm, in synchronized footsteps, the young man's arm around his girl's shoulder, hers around his waist.

From between Sugar Reef Bar and Bajan Jewels, the tamarind-seed beggar leapt out of the alleyway in front of the lovers, holding out his hand.

The young man, wearing a white t-shirt and cutoffs, dismissed him with a wave and kept walking, never missing a step. His girlfriend—something told me they were not yet married—clung closer to him, but her footsteps never lost the rhythm of his. The beggar walked backward with them, down a curb, up another, yammering away about his good-luck tree. Finally, in front of a parked car, he stepped out of their way, followed for a few more futile steps, lagged, gave up. The lovers moved on, leaving him standing in the middle of the empty street, holding out his hand.

The beggar did not insult them, as he had me, did not accuse them of rape, pillage, or plunder.

The couple, snuggling, passed me standing on the hotel steps. In another minute, Bay Street was moribund once more.

But the beggar still stood halfway down the block, glowing green and orange. When he saw me, he grinned, his front tooth gleaming in the neon. His eyes bulged tree-frog-like. He stretched out his hand, presumably with the tamarind seed in it. "Tief," he called, sucking his gums.

"You want to buy me seed now? Twenty dollars now, Mr. Tief."

I wanted to throttle him. I wanted Annie to hear the man screaming, to step onto our balcony and see me thrashing him to a pulp. But when I glanced up, the balcony was empty.

"Tief! Bad luck not to buy me seed! Bad, bad, Mr. Tief! You tief me island, you pay de price!"

Saying nothing, I retreated into the lobby. My tormentor stood outside the hotel door, his face pressed to the glass, his hand cupped, taunting me. The woman clerk had returned, yawning, blinking sleep from her eyes. "Don't pay attention to him," she said. "He's harmless. Sometimes he runs around naked, but he hasn't hurt anyone yet."

I walked past the bar and the pool, down the steps to the beach—dark but for the hazy glow of a gibbous moon. It was just light enough to see the message written on an old fishing skiff, drawn up onto the sand and now used for advertising: EAT AT SHORTY'S.

Didn't Annie remember how poor we were the first time around? Didn't she see how much our Schwab account had grown? Didn't she realize how brilliant I was? What was wrong with a little appreciation? A simple thank-you. A nice second-honeymoon grind.

I decided she was the most ungrateful woman I had ever known. The most ungrateful on the planet. I glanced at the moon. *In the whole cosmos.*

From the shadows I watched the tourist couple sitting on the edge of the jetty playing kissy-face. Even with the moon half-full, the sky smoldered with stars.

Most women would kill to trade places with my ungrateful wife, I thought. They sure as hell wouldn't come down to Barbados on their twentieth anniversary just to slime their stupid face, roll over, and fall asleep. They'd be *thrilled* to be married to Global B.

To hell with her.

As I walked back down the beach, the moon retreated behind a nugget of cloud. But it was still light enough to see my own solitary footsteps in the sand, already half-dissolved by the incoming tide.

"I'm still going to Fire Mountain," I told her the next morning. We had talked about the distillery tour. "You want to come?"

"I think I'll hang around the beach and read," she said, not letting up. "That's what honeymoons are for."

"I thought honeymoons are for having sex with your wife."

"Conserve your energy for puts and calls."

I took a taxi clockwise up the coast. Halfway up the island, at Sandy Point, the driver turned inland toward St. Thomas Parish, climbing the bib of what might have been an ancient volcano, now carpeted with undulating sugar cane. In the center of the island, on a lush brow, loomed the vaneless ruins of an eighteenth-century sugar mill, casting a ragged shadow. Beyond that nestled a complex of four pale-yellow, wood-plank buildings and two smaller, red-tile-roofed stone buildings. I took in the scene with a keen entrepreneurial eye, wondering what opportunities in this undeveloped swatch of fecundity might await a business genius such as myself.

I imagined the marketing potential of this hidden treasure: humble folks, descendants of slaves, applying skills passed down through generations, toiling with pride in virtual obscurity. I liked its romantic quaintness—like those "We'll leave the light on for you" motel commercials.

As the taxi coiled down the slope, I envisioned an advertising concept for Fire Mountain Estates rum. Like most successful campaigns, it would be profoundly simple. One word popped into my brain: *Still. Still*, with all its connotations. I rubbed my hands, gleeful at its understated brilliance. *Still.* I sat on the edge of the seat, my head out the window, breathing the redolent breeze. For a moment, I even forgot about Annie.

"It's beautiful," I told the driver.

"Yes, suh."

"You like Fire Mountain rum?"

"Oh, yes, suh. Yes."

"If you wait for me, I'll buy you a bottle."

The driver's eyes lit up in the mirror. "Fine, suh. Fine, fine. I'll wait as long as you want."

Global B.

"No one knows for certain the origin of the word *rum*," said Ms. Lilah Pett, the perky docent, "but it may come from the Latin word for sugar cane: *saccharum officinarum*." She was small but sturdy, with a smooth, almond-shaded complexion. Her short reddish-brown hair, swept back on the sides, covered her ears except for the lobes, from which hung pearl teardrop earrings. She wore a sleek blue dress patterned with white and yellow hibiscuses, a pearl necklace, and fashionable canvas sandals. Her toes were polished clear. She was pretty, with thin Caucasian features. In the corporate scheme of things, I saw her more as a media-relations person than a tour guide.

For taking people around on factory visits, I pictured a blacker, thicker-skinned woman dressed in traditional billowing dress and native head wrap. Barefoot, maybe. Mammy type, huggable—like those plush, roving characters in Disney World.

"Lovable mouse," I said under my breath.

"Mouse?" squeaked Ms. Pett.

The visitors' glances darted around the ground.

"No, no," I stammered, embarrassed. "I was just thinking aloud."

Ms. Pett cleared her throat. "Or the name could come from the fact that plantation owners gave rum to their slaves to cure their head colds—the French word for cold being *rhume*."

I was among a group of six visitors taking the 11 A.M. tour—this, our first stop, being a replication of a colonial distillery.

"In 1687," said Lilah Pett, "the British Royal Navy officially adopted a pint of rum as their sailors' daily ration—a reward for good behavior."

"Good behavior," I muttered, suddenly remembering Annie.

"In the old days of wind-powered mills, slaves would cut cane with machetes, bring it to the mill in ox carts, and feed the stalks twice through the grinding wheel to extract its juice."

Lilah Pett's voice was juicy and sweet, and it oozed out her sunny white teeth. I imagined her naked, delivering a lecture on the history of the colonial wench, her arms flailing like windmill vanes, her perky rump undulating in the breeze. I decided that should I indeed divert some of my NASDAQ riches into this fertile and deserving enterprise, Ms. Lilah Pett would move up fast in my organization.

"From the crushing wheel," she continued, gesturing to three large caldrons, "the fresh juice ran down a sluice to the boiling house, where it was ladled into cast-iron pots and cooked over an open fire of dried cane stalks and wood. As the liquid thickened, lime was added to precipitate unwanted impurities and aid fermentation."

Ms. Pett was very groomed, very professional. Even in the still-steamy late-morning air, not one of her hairs was wilted or out of place, not a single thread of her dress wrinkled. Her only concession to the heat was a patina of sweat across the bridge of her nose, and even that had a come-hither quality. I was surprised. Somehow the image of fat fruit vendors balancing stalks of bananas on their heads had lodged in the back of my mind. But Ms. Pett was a modern, articulate businesswoman—dressed more for a board meeting than a trip through cane fields—and I found that a pleasant surprise, indeed.

I had the impression that Lilah Pett was eminently rational. A clear, logical thinker—unlike another woman I happened to know. I imagined that an idea would enter Ms. Pett's brain, evaporate to its essence, and, through a process of precise heating and cooling, distill to an unclouded conclusion. I was certain she would see the illogic of, in the very same sentence, sympathizing with a beggar and then accusing him of being a machete murderer. I believed Ms. Pett would stare agog at my Charles Schwab account statement. Perhaps she would even faint. I believed Ms. Pett was herself wondering why Fire Mountain Estates had allowed itself to remain obscure and was longing for a man of my superior money-making skills to rescue the tiny firm from oblivion. I believed that Ms. Pett was, in two words, sexually frustrated.

"After most of the liquid has been boiled out," she explained, "the result is molasses."

When I pictured molasses I could not prevent my wife from coming to mind. Thick, gunky, 85 percent dissolved solids. Impossible to swallow. No kick, no buzz, no reason, no logic.

I had never cheated on Annie, but sometimes she made it a tough day's work. Sometimes it was like cutting cane for fourteen hours in the predatory sun, hitching myself to an ox cart, hauling load after load back to the mill, only to get my schmuck caught under a grinding stone.

"Next we'll go to our working distillery, to show you how fermentation and distillation is accomplished today, here at Fire Mountain Estates."

We followed Ms. Pett through a yard, into a hangar-like building, and up a flight of creaky stairs, where we lined up on a quavering catwalk, overlooking six stainless-steel tanks—an armada glinting under a fluorescent sky.

"Over 50 percent of the molasses is fermentable sugar," she continued, her hip pressed into the railing, beads of sweat glimmering in the cup of her throat. "Here, we add our proprietary yeast formula to the finest molasses imported from Trinidad. The resulting mixture is known as *wash*. The yeast consumes the sugar in the wash to produce alcohol and carbon dioxide and heat. In approximately three days, the wash is fermented into alcohol, which we then call *wine*. The wine is pumped to the distillation building, where we will go next."

We went downstairs and, passing through a gangway, entered another building, where gleaming pipes webbed two-story distillation towers.

"Other small distilleries use one or two columns to

purify their rum," said Ms. Pett, "but we at Fire Mountain Estates incorporate *three* copper-clad columns to assure you of the finest premium spirits available throughout the West Indies. A truly unique taste sensation."

I wondered what kind of sensation it would be to dribble a few drops of Fire Mountain Heavenly Dark rum onto Ms. Pett's heavenly dark thighs as she bubbled spiritedly under my sensational column. Fiery Ms. Pett. Hot, sweaty, premium, but hopefully not yeasty, Ms. Lilah Pett. Gazing hornily at her, that's what I was thinking. Blame Annie.

"In the still, heat under pressure is applied to the fermented wine. The alcohol vapors are cooled in a condensing vat, pumped into the next column, and so on. By the time the distilled rum leaves the third still, it is 94 percent alcohol by volume."

Fiery, tangy, *pressurized* Ms. Pett.

"Finally, water is added to this overproofed spirit to reduce its strength. Usually, the alcohol content winds up to be 45 to 55 percent. Any questions?"

"What are the taps used for at the bottom of the columns?" a fellow with bushy white eyebrows asked.

Ms. Pett glanced around the group. "Does anyone know the answer?" Getting everyone involved. I liked that.

"To remove non-productive impurities," I ventured. Again, Annie came to mind.

Lilah Pett took a long, curious look at me. I felt the other tourists' admiring stares.

"That's exactly right," said Ms. Pett, she of the copper-clad, finest-tasting, most premium gams available throughout the West Indies. "Are you in the same business?"

"Nope. Just read a lot."

"You like rum?"

"I like yours. I like yours a lot."

"We have a saying here: the more informed you are, the better Fire Mountain tastes." Ms. Pett rose up on her toes.

She led us to the far end of the building. They let me walk in front, right behind our lovely docent. "The stills yield about one gallon of rum for every fifteen gallons of fermented wash," she explained. "Distilling the first part of a batch produces the strongest spirits, or *high wines*, and the last part the weakest, or *low wines*. We separate and remove these *heads* and *tails* and collect the in-betweens, called *seconds*, which we then age and blend. Before moving on to the aging warehouse, are there any questions?"

"What are those glass pipes for?" the wife of the bushy-eyebrowed man asked, pointing to long vertical tubes at the base of each distillation column. "They look like big coffee urns."

Ms. Pett glanced my way.

"Sight glasses," I offered. "If I'm right, they have beads in them that float or sink depending on the alcohol content of the rum."

"Quite right, indeed. Right again. Three beads each." Ms. Pett's eyelashes danced a silent samba. "Let's move along, shall we?" she told the group, without taking her eyes off her star pupil.

We walked down a gravel path, through a weedy lot, to a stone warehouse. Ms. Pett motioned us aside, to get out of the way of a forklift truck that came rumbling out of accordion doors. Diesel exhaust rose and burled. The wife of the bushy-eyebrowed man coughed a raspy hack.

We went inside. Barrels were stacked to twenty-foot-high ceilings. Row after row of racks, barrel upon barrel. When the diesel smell dissipated, the aroma of tannin and aging rum hung thick on the mossy stones.

"We store almost two thousand casks within these old walls," said Ms. Pett. "A quarter-million liters of the finest rum in the world."

I licked my lips.

"The rum is aged from six months to four years. We import oak barrels from distilleries in the U.S. and Canada that have been used to store whiskey, bourbon, and cognac. We then singe the inside of the barrels for charcoal flavoring and, after filling, mark them with the date of the batch, lot number, and percentage of alcohol. The bungs, or stoppers, are made of local poplar, due to its superior sealing ability."

I imagined myself bunging Ms. Pett so hard and fast that I singed the inside of her barrel, imparting a smoky, savory flavor.

"The casks are stored on their sides, as you see, and rotated weekly to maximize the rum's contact with the oak."

I would certainly rotate Ms. Pett.

She moved through the rum cathedral. I stayed close behind, feeling the warmth of her flesh, inhaling her lilac cologne.

We made a brief stop at the blending building, then returned to the visitors' center, where the tour had begun.

"And now for the best part," said Lilah Pett, standing before a varnished mahogany bar, light glinting off her lips. She gestured to a dozen gleaming brandy snifters, lined up on the counter. "Here you can sample our light, medium, and Heavenly Dark rums." She nodded at the bartender. "And if you dare, try our rare, fifteen-year-old overproofed Extra Dark. But be prepared for a jolt, because it's 70 percent alcohol!"

The bartender filled the bottom of a snifter with two-year-old, medium-gold rum. Ms. Pett lifted it to the sunlight. "To thoroughly enjoy the experience of tasting fine rum, first hold it up to judge its clearness and color." She swirled it gently. "This creates aroma in the glass. Then, take a deep breath, exhale, hold the snifter to your nose." She demonstrated. "Slowly inhale the delightful vapors. Assess its delicate and subtle aroma." She ended with a tiny sip and saucy half-smile. She glanced sidelong at yours truly. "Eating beforehand always improves the experience. Ice water afterward cools the palate."

I needed my palate cooled—big time. A drop of rum had escaped the corner of Ms. Pett's lips and threatened to dribble down her chin. Without taking her eyes off her number-one student, she licked it, then wiped the crease of her mouth with a shimmering fingertip.

Global B's boiler was about to blow.

The bartender poured me three samples, and I gulped them down in single swallows without glancing at them—never mind holding them up to the light, swirling, and sniffing. Then I asked for a shot of the overproofed Extra Dark. I held that on my tongue for a moment, feeling the burn, then, clacking the snifter onto the mahogany, swallowed hard, held my breath, and braced. A second later the percussion came, fumes rose up my throat, through my palate and brain, and out the top of my bald pate.

I held the snifter out for an encore, and another after that.

With the rum blending in my gut—eight shots in all—and their vapors swirling delightfully in my skull, I got up the courage to approach Ms. Pett, who was shaking the last of her visitors' hands. She was only fifteen feet away, but it seemed a long way to go. It was like I was at a singles bar, walking across the parquet to ask the sexiest girl in the place to dance. If it worked, I'd be a hero to my poker buddies, but if she said no, my life as I knew it was over.

I staggered slightly, found my balance, stopped to assess the situation, wondering if my head was too shiny, wondering, idiotically, if my breath smelled like liquor. I silently rehearsed what I was going to say. Finally, I pulled up short, reminding myself that I wasn't just some ordinary tourist schlemiel off a cruise ship. I wasn't a shirtless beggar with a phony ten-dollar tamarind seed. Hell, no. What I was, was... *Global B.*

Here were the salient points of the deal I silently and somewhat tipsily negotiated with my future offshore corporation. If perky Ms. Pett showed the kind of interest in me that I hoped she would, I would recommend to my board of directors to promote her to vice president in charge of something or other. If, on the other hand, the docent had worked me into a froth to no avail, I would aggressively pursue the purchase of this small distillery until the day I died for the sheer pleasure of seeing Ms. Pett dressed in native head wrap, shoelessly leading dumb-question-asking tourists around the distillery *while balancing bundles of bananas on her head.*

Blame Annie.

Blame Annie for the fact that the fate of tailored, highly professional, modern, logical, luscious, and thoroughly delectable Ms. Lilah Pett now rested solely, completely, utterly, and absolutely in the hands of her perky-rumped response.

She held out her hand as I approached. My palms were

sweating like evaporation coils. She could have just said thank you and have a good day, and let it go at that, but she did not. What she said was, "You're the smartest, most virile-looking man I have ever met. The top of your head is so handsomely slick!"

I rattled my skull and stared at her dumbly.

She repeated herself: "Thank you for coming. Do you have any other questions, sir?"

All right, maybe the rum was stronger than I thought.

"Do you like me?" I stammered.

"Sir?"

I cleared my throat. The room began to swirl, just as the rum had swirled against the sides of the snifters.

"Do I like you?" she repeated.

"I do." I waited. The visitor center was listing about 45 degrees, a sloop in a Force-12 hurricane.

"Sir, are you all right?"

I raised a finger. "Why can't I find Fire Mountain rum in the States?" I glanced around for a porthole to open.

"Oh, our visitors ask us that all the time. It's all about quality, you see. The best rum takes time to mellow and mature. If we suddenly started selling in huge quantities, we would have to release barrels before their proper aging period. I'm not saying it would be bad rum, it would just be different. We happen to be fond of what we have. We don't really want anything different."

"Don't I what?" I asked after a beat.

She grabbed my shoulder to steady me. "Do you want to sit down, sir?"

I looked around, wondering which of the Lilah Petts was talking.

"Better come to the bench with me, sir."

"I'm all right."

"Are you sure? That's strong rum. I saw you drink all those samples."

"You saw me? You like me?"

"I like you fine, sir. Won't you sit down, though?"

"O.K.," I agreed.

Then I vomited all over her.

"You should see how stupid you look," Annie said as she fed me spoonfuls of Pepto Bismol. I lay propped up under the hotel sheet. My head felt like a wet goat was sitting on it.

"Do you love me?" I wanted to know.

"Do you think I could live with this head and not love it?"

"I made a real mess."

"Nothing that can't be fixed. Everything can be fixed."

"I ruined her dress. I don't remember much after hitting the floor."

"I gave them your credit card number and told them to help themselves. Notice I didn't say *our* credit card number."

"Will you sleep with me tonight?"

She kissed the top of my skull. "Of course, sweet man. I'm sorry about last night and this morning."

"What happened?"

"It's just that Fire Mountain is about *us*. You and me— not Global B. Barbados is *ours*, not Charles Schwab's."

"We were so poor. Don't you remember?"

"Of course I remember. Those days were awful. But it's what we had."

"Them and each other."

She squeezed my nose. "Now you're getting it, moron boy."

"I made a jerk of myself at Fire Mountain."

"That's because you are a jerk."

"I love Barbados."

"Me too."

I clutched her hand to my breastbone. She kissed my knuckles.

"I'm done with rum forever."

"A little's not bad. Next time, try it in a punch. A punch would be good for you."

"O.K., I get it."

"You do? You finally get it?"

"You know what I've been thinking?"

She tilted her head.

"I was thinking maybe I'll sell our stocks and take our profits."

"All of them?"

I shrugged.

"Didn't Neal say at this rate NASDAQ will be 7,500 by July?"

"It's O.K. I think we made enough."

She squeezed my hand. "I think you're making the right decision."

"As soon as we get home."

"Why wait?" She handed me my cell phone. "If it's one call Charles Schwab will answer, it's Global B's."

At midnight—after I had sold all our tech stocks, taken a nice snooze, and Annie and I enjoyed a lobster dinner

across the street, then returned to the hotel to make love—
we decided to skinny dip in the ocean.

"Just like our honeymoon," I said.

"Just like."

We padded downstairs wearing nothing but towels. The
night clerk smiled at us sleepily and returned to her magazine. The pool shimmered, reflecting onto a thicket of
hibiscus bushes. Tree frogs were in full chorus. A white-
and-gray cat meatloafed on a stack of beach chairs, its eyes
miniature moons. Palm fronds rustled under a wisp of east-
erly breeze. Heat lightning pulsed on the horizon, illumi-
nating nothing but itself.

We draped our towels over Shorty's beached advertising
skiff and went into the water, me sprinting rambunctiously
and Annie easing herself in. Neck deep, we hugged. I
scooped her up and kissed her breast.

"You're a wild man."

"You look the same as when we got married. *Better.*"

"You have a lot less hair."

"But you love me."

"I sure do."

I heard something. Annie heard it too, and it startled her.
"What's that?" She turned to follow my gaze.

I thought I saw something moving in Shorty's skiff. I
squinted into the darkness, holding Annie tighter. She
clutched my neck. "Something in the boat there," I
whispered.

"A dog, probably."

But it was the ragged beggar who rose from inside the
boat, vampire-like. "You wake me up!" he scolded, shaking
his fist.

"Oh no."

"Bad luck, bad luck to wake de Rastaman!" he shouted, climbing out of his coffin. "You pay price for waking de Rasta!" he blasted, grabbing our towels. "You trow property in man's house, you lose property! Squatter's rights!"

"He's stealing our towels," she gasped. "And our room key."

He ran away and disappeared down the beach, our towels contrailing behind his bony shoulders.

"Now what do we do?"

"I suppose it's too late to buy one of his seeds," I said.

She squeezed me. "My business genius."

"Well, I suppose we can either worry about it or keep swimming."

She shrugged. "Maybe the towels will show up later."

"Maybe they will," I said, kissing her other breast, "and maybe they won't."

"I'll bet you miss your cell phone now, don't you?"

"Not really."

"You still love me," she wanted to know, "even though we sold all our stock?"

I jackknifed my legs, and we dropped under the water. I got my head between her thighs, and when I stood again, she was riding my shoulders, a sea beast rising from the phosphorescent tide. She screamed with fake fright, then glee.

"Nothing to hold onto anymore," she said, groping my noggin.

I plowed up-shore until the water reached my knees.

She grabbed my eyebrows. "Whee!"

I started running, making huge splashes.

The beggar reappeared from between two shacks. When he saw us galloping through the surf, he ran alongside, on the beach, our towels vortexing behind him. "Bad luck to wake Rasta!" he screamed ecstatically.

"Ride 'em, cowboy!" Annie shouted, holding onto my eyebrow with one hand, thwacking my head with the other.

"Buy me seed! Buy me seed!" yelled the ragamuffin.

"She still loves me!" I exclaimed.

"I still do!" she bellowed, slapping my scalp.

"Me too! Me too!" shrieked the beggar, dropping his shorts and, with me and my wife, stampeding naked under the moon.

El Max

I KNEW THE BUS DRIVER WAS GOING TO BE TROUBLE.
He evidently had no first name, but his last name was
Lopez, and he was small and angular, and his eyes were
round and black like a rat's. He never looked at you but
stared out the windshield, even though the bus was still
parked and it was the middle of the night. He didn't respond when you said *holá,* just tapped his gnarly fingers on
the steering wheel, gazed out at the dim lot, and occasionally picked gook out of his eyes. He refused to budge.

We had landed after midnight, but some of the group
were coming in on a separate plane, and there was no
telling when they'd get to Havana. But our bus driver refused to take the first part of the group to our hotel and return for the others. We had been traveling for almost
twenty-four hours. After delays in Chicago, Toronto, and
Montreal, we had finally taken off in a blinding ice storm,
terrorized by the paroxysms of a 1950s Aeroflot Soviet jet-
liner with chewing gum for hors d'oeuvres and rivets. We
were too exhausted even to cheer when we finally touched
down, and now the son of a bitch wanted us to sit on the
bus and wait for the other plane. He wouldn't budge.

We knew his name was Lopez because our HavanaTur
guide, an affable young man in his early twenties, whose

name was Roberto Baez—but who asked us to call him Bob—kept yelling at him in Spanish to take us to the hotel. Most of us did not speak Spanish, but we got the gist of it, and every once in a while Bob would sprinkle his exhortations with the name *Lopez*, so that's how we knew. One of us who did speak a little Spanish said Bob called the driver a "dog's anus," but Lopez only replied by staring at his reflection in the windshield and scratching his butt.

After each vain appeal, Bob turned to us with a forced smile and, in pretty good English, said, "We assure you, your friends are almost here, and we will be on our way extremely shortly. We know it has been an extremely long day, and extremely shortly you will be asleep on your extremely soft pillow in your hotel. We welcome you extremely much to our extremely beautiful city, which you cannot see now, but you will surely see in the daytime."

Then he turned again to the driver and—for our benefit—pretended to engage in good-natured banter but was really calling him combinations of names that included animals and orifices. But Lopez still wouldn't budge.

So right away I knew he was going to be trouble.

I'm cranky when I'm tired. Also when I'm hungry, thirsty, have missed any episodes of *The Apprentice*, or am visiting any country that doesn't have Starbucks or macaroni and cheese. Long about one-thirty, after another of Bob's futile go-rounds with Lopez, I had had enough. I had been a courteous American for an hour and a half—way longer than average. Being a man of action, I got up to offer Lopez a bribe, when the long arm of the law, my wife, pulled me back by my elbow skin. "Sit," she said. When I looked down, my glance was met by the same malevolent gaze as Christ's detractors in Mel Gibson's *Passion*. I did not actually see the movie, but I saw enough excerpts on TV to guess the main idea. When they showed Jesus with deep, bloody lacerations all over his face and body, I thought: *cat owner*. Oh, great, so in addition to killing the son of God, Jews were also responsible for not declawing their pets. That's what I thought. Sue me.

Five hours in an ice storm with hurricane winds on a Soviet airplane with a beaded curtain for a toilet door and krill for meal service cannot compare with the terror induced by my wife's gaze, usually reserved for when I say something mean but truthful about her nephew, the thirty-year-old Nintendo wiz. I sat back down.

"You're not going to spend two weeks in a Havana jail," she hissed.

"How come?"

"It might distract me."

Our companion plane arrived from Canada at four-thirty in the morning, and by the time that group was interrogated and frisked, it was dawn over Cuba, but we were at last on our way. Havana is lovely in the morning, assuming your underpants haven't risen into your small intestine.

On the plus side, our hotel, the Parque Central in La Habana Vieja, was clean and luxurious. The Dutch always run first-rate accommodations, to make up for the fact that you have to dig up tulip bulbs in the fall and replant them every spring. They probably also felt guilty because in Cuba you can't eat without involving pig parts, although this is not the fault of Dutch people but of Fidel Castro, who, every time the Americans talk about lifting the embargo, opens his big yap. Not a pork lover myself, I had to remind myself that Hemingway would not only have eaten the oinkers, he would have shot them. In that order.

At eleven-thirty, a knock woke us up. "It is I, Bob."

For a moment, I forgot who Bob was. Havana does not yet have peep holes or other basic security devices, probably because they do not have many lawyers. Shirtless, I cracked the door and peeked at our guide's grinning kisser. "Bob," he repeated. "Might I come in?"

"My wife's still sleeping."

"I'm awake," Annie said behind me. She dashed into the bathroom with her clothes, afraid she might miss an excursion that involved purchasing carved coconut heads. "Don't let them leave without us."

Bob glanced up and down the hallway, then stepped in. "It's an extremely beautiful hotel, don't you think? They are holding breakfast until noon today, in honor of your extremely late arrival. Excellent pork." The front of his guayabera bulged weirdly, as if his own breakfast had consisted of a cinder block.

"What can I do for you?"

"Lopez is a scoundrel. A worm's earhole. Complete turtle excretion...if I understand the term correctly."

"You're doing fine."

"My brother Alberto, a police *capitano*, would like to arrest him for being such a goat's ass." He raised an eyebrow. "He would take care of him extremely firmly, I assure you. No further visitors would be so inconvenienced."

I motioned to the chair. He pulled it out and sat, the bulge under his shirt rising to his chest.

"Unfortunately, my brother's hands are tied. Do I use the phrase correctly?" He lowered his voice. "Lopez is a good communist. Head of his CDR—Committee for the

Defense of the Revolution." He lowered his voice even more, and his forehead furled. "He has broken bread with El Maximo. I myself am not political. I stay out of it. But Lopez is a pig's nostril. I am here to give you advice. Be careful what you and your friends say on the bus. The villain reports everything."

"I don't have any friends."

"Ah, I see. Extremely wise. Your wife, then."

Annie popped out of the bathroom. "His wife what?"

"Don't talk in front of Lopez."

"And, good heavens, never offer him a bribe!"

She glanced at me and whistled soundlessly.

Bob grimaced, the cinder block digging into his spleen.

"I think Bob brought us a box lunch. Pork, I'll bet."

"Oh," our guide said, pretending he had just remembered the hidden package. "Oh, yes, this." He motioned to the bulge. "Do you mind?" He slipped the bundle out of his guayabera. He plopped a filthy, fat manila envelope onto his lap and took a breath. "Your visa says you are a writer."

"A bad one," I assured him.

He patted the grease-spotted envelope. "I am wondering if you would read my novel. Not here, of course. Take it home and read it when you are relaxed."

"You want me to smuggle your manuscript out of Cuba?"

"I thought perhaps, and only if you like it, you might show it to a publisher—"

"We'll get into trouble."

Bob flicked a finger. "My brother would not allow that. Do not worry." His glance fell on my Star of David necklace. "We have a secret weapon." He whispered, "We, too, are of Hebrew persuasion."

Annie's toes did a little conga. "You? Jewish?"

"And Alberto, naturally." He chortled, "Fidel thinks he is, too." He paused and looked around. "Not that we want him. But it comes in extremely handy. My brother is teaching him Yiddish. Alberto doesn't speak a word of it. He makes it all up. You should hear the Bearded One trying to talk like a Jew. Extremely amusing."

"Of course we'll take your novel," Annie piped. "And my husband is a *very good* writer." Always there when I need her.

"Wonderful! Wonderful!" He handed her the package. "You can tell no one it is mine, naturally," he whispered. "I left my name off it entirely."

I took it from Annie and handed it back. "Sorry. Out of the question. Anyhow, I'm disliked in the trade."

She took it back and buried it at the bottom of my suitcase. "It's in good hands."

"Written entirely in English," Bob puffed. "Printed for ease of reading."

"*Longhand?*" she exclaimed.

"I will be glad to divide any money with you fifty–fifty, if I'm phrasing that correctly?" He got up and offered me his hand.

Annie took it. "Not necessary, we assure you. We're glad to help an oppressed artist."

"You will have a glorious ten days in Cuba, with me as your guide."

"I have no doubt."

"Well, *I* have a doubt," I said, reaching for the manuscript. But before I could shove it back into his shirt, he was out the door.

I turned to Annie. "I thought you said my being in jail would be a distraction."

"This is different. He's probably a literary genius. A Cuban J. D. Salinger. Think of his determination and hardship, writing it out longhand. He's *Jewish*."

"Apparently so is Fidel, but I wouldn't trust him with my pork chop."

"All right, if they make a fuss—which I highly doubt—*I'll* go to jail. How's that?"

"It doesn't work that way. Do the names Julius and Ethel Rosenberg ring a bell?"

"You're on vacation. Relax." She kissed my chin. "Who knows, maybe he'll dedicate it to you. That would be something, wouldn't it? Anyhow, they shoot you here, they don't electrocute you."

"It must be nice being married to a love-sick imbecile."

"It comes in extremely handy. Now get dressed and let's go for breakfast. Then I want to buy something shiny." She suddenly looked worried. "Communists sell shiny things, don't they?"

After lunch the bus was waiting. Bob had held the front seats for Annie and me. The other people in the group drilled us a look. One woman in particular, a manicurist from Detroit with six-inch fingernails painted to depict important events in the life of black leaders—one pinky being Marcus Garvey's parade down Lenox Avenue, and a thumb Martin Luther King's "I Have a Dream" speech on the National Mall—cut me a snarl, possibly sensing race-related shenanigans. I knew that unless I got on her good side, I would never leave Cuba with both eyes. Nevertheless, I sat. May as well enjoy the scenery while you still have depth perception.

"Today we are going to Veradero Beach," Bob reminded us, as Lopez swung the bus onto the Malecón. "We will have lunch and enjoy the sun." He sliced me a wink. "Cubans themselves are not permitted on the beach." He glanced at Lopez accusatorially. "Only tourists." I did not wink back.

Twenty minutes later I told Annie I had to go to the bathroom.

"So go. What do you want from me?"

"I have to pass that woman."

"Protect your eyes."

"What if she goes for the family jewels?"

"One hand on your face, one on your crotch. This is not brain surgery."

"It'll look like I'm afraid of her."

"You are afraid of her."

"People will think I'm weak and eat off my plate."

"Think pork."

"Point taken."

"Besides," she whispered, "we've got Roberto's brother."

I smiled at Bob and, yes, winked. I got up and walked gingerly to the back, whistling "Candy Man" by Sammy Davis Jr. Other than her staring at my hand covering my crotch, there were no incidents...until I tried to leave the bathroom. The door stuck. I mean, S-T-U-C-K. I wiggled the sliding latch and jammed it back hard. *Nada.* I pulled it back and got my knee up and pushed my other leg against the commode and heaved, but the door didn't budge. It occurred to me that the Detroit woman was leaning on it from the other side. Perhaps she had recruited the other members of our group, many of whom had wanted to sit in the front seat. Perhaps some of them were familiar with my writing. Meanwhile, the bus was barreling down the coastal road, picking up speed, jouncing me like an asymmetrical Cuban-lottery ball, and the windowless three-by-three cubical, which was directly over the diesel engine, was getting ten degrees hotter per minute. And guess what? I'm claustrophobic.

Sometimes I get panic attacks when my sheets are tucked in too tight, even when I'm not in bed. If you've ever had a claustrophobia attack, you know they are terrifying, degrading, and make you regret all those times you promised to write something nice about a hotel or restaurant just to get a free room or food, knowing full well you were going to stiff them, review-wise. You're sure you're going to pass out and poop in your pants, and that strangers will rifle through your wallet and find a picture of your parakeet. You're also sure no one else on the bus will have to go to the bathroom all the way to Veradero, and your wife will fall asleep, which she likes to do, and you'll pass out with your head in the potty, and it will get so hot in there that by the time anyone notices you're missing, your skull will have shrunk to the size and density of a nutmeg.

It was time to pound.

With the engine roaring like an F-16 or my lawn mower after Annie's nephew borrowed it and forgot to put in oil, I wasn't sure if anyone could hear me. I took no chances. I pounded and yelled, yelled and pounded, my panic attack in full shock and awe. The louder I screamed and whacked the door, the more spiritedly Lopez revved the engine. The bus was going faster and faster, the bathroom was getting hotter and hotter, my breaths were harder and harder, and my temples percussed like 10,000-pound bunker-busters.

The son of a bitch must have known I had Bob's novel.

"Help! I'm stuck!"

Bob yelled back at me. "Pull the latch back!"

Annie shouted, "Take deep breaths and slow down your alpha waves, like Dr. Luce taught you."

"It's hot! I can't breathe!"

"Close your eyes and imagine yourself lying in a lovely meadow next to a country lake!"

"Tell Lopez to stop the bus! I'm going to pass out from the fumes!"

"I'll be right back!" Roberto hollered.

"Hurry!"

The bus went faster.

"You still there, honey?!" Annie shouted.

"Kill Lopez!"

"Roberto's talking to him! Close your eyes and pretend you're listening to Handel's *Water Music*."

"Kill the commie motherfucker!"

Finally, finally, Bob ran back. "He won't stop! He said the nation depends on him to arrive on time! It is a matter of prestige! But don't worry, we will get you out!"

He shoved something into the door jam. "I have a pen. If only it will go—"

But, writing instruments being useless when you really need them, it was too fat to reach the lock tongue.

"Do you have a tire iron?!" I shouted.

No answer. Annie might have been interpreting.

"A tire iron!" Roberto confirmed. "To fix flat tires! Of course!"

"*Pry* me the hell out of here!"

"It's with the spare tire! Under the bus! We would have to stop!"

Lopez went faster.

"I love you, honey!"

I felt woozy. The rumble of the diesel receded, approached, receded again. Annie's voice sounded tinny and far away—even more than usual. My vision blurred. I could feel my carotid artery in my toes. My tongue was the size and consistency of a Vienna salami, my flesh cold and lifeless. I lost sense of time. The walls began to swirl. My knees gave way. I remembered being born.

Then, as if in a dream, I saw Martin Luther King slip through the door crack.

A moment later, the latch slammed back, the door jolted open, and the manicurist from Detroit filled the doorway. "You all right now, sweet baby!" she trumpeted, fanning me with her nails. Fresh air whooshed over my bloodless mug. "Charmaine set you free!"

She hefted me to my feet and hauled me down the aisle, pushing Bob and Annie aside, shouting, "Get outta the way, we marching to freedom!" She deposited me in my front-row seat, warning Annie, "Take care of him. Men with good nails don't grow on trees." Then she turned to Lopez and bared her teeth, but he was too busy picking gook out of his eye to notice.

The day we left Cuba I noticed my Star of David pendant missing. It was a stamped, fourteen-karat gold-plated cheapy, but my Aunt Rose had bought it for me in Israel, so I liked it. Anyhow, my taste tends to run toward the cheap—not in the Donald Trump sense of the word, but in the inexpensive sense of the word. I lose things a lot when traveling, and this time it was my necklace. Still, after breakfast I offhandedly asked Roberto if anyone had turned it in. He said no and even though I assured him it was junk jewelry, he seemed extremely concerned and checked with the concierge. Shaking his head solemnly, he took me aside and whispered, "Do you think you lost it on the bus?"

"It's possible, I guess."

He pursed his lips. "I see."

"You do?"

"Lopez must have found it and kept it, that thieving sheep rectum. Well, we'll see about that." He lowered his voice even more. "You still have my...merchandise?"

I nodded.

"I await your verdict with pines and noodles. You can reach me through my brother."

When, a few weeks later, I finished reading Bob's man-uscript, I handed it to my wife. Annie is always trying to sign over our home and other assets to foreign people who say they love America. Our Polish cleaning lady, for exam-ple, is an indefatigable young woman who hunts down dirt like Purvis hunted down Dillinger. Believe me, I like her, too. But I still don't see why I should marry her to make her a citizen. I also like our gardener, Raoul, even though he formed an offshore corporation to launder the money we pay him. Or Viktor, our Croatian painter, whose rehab treatments Annie offered to subsidize, forcing us to cash in the savings bonds I got at my bar mitzvah, and who's only on Step Two.

So I knew she really, really wanted to like Bob's novel. She had been watching me from the corner of her eye as I leafed through the manuscript, stone-faced. Finally, it was hers.

A couple of days later, she handed it back. "It's horrible."

"What? Not worth rotting in a tropical prison for?"

"As near as I can figure, it's *Fiddler on the Roof*—without a fiddler or a roof."

"Or a shred of talent. In itself not enough to keep it off the *Times'* bestseller list, mind you."

Her eyes lit up. "You're not saying there's actually hope for—"

I hefted the manuscript. "Cat litter."

She deflated. "What are you going to tell Bob?"

"*Me?*"

"Technically, he gave it to you, not me. Let him down easy. Promise?"

I had her. She had lurched unwittingly into my trap. What she didn't know was that, at that very moment, hunkered in my desk drawer was a letter I had plucked from the mailbox yesterday, while she had been out shopping for something nice for herself.

My Dear *Señor* Gary

We are knowing about your stoling star and we opened a file on your theft. We will not rest, we will never rest, until we solve this badly crime. Our nation depends on us. It is a matter of prestige.

Yours truly,

Cpt. Alberto Paul Baez (Captain)
District Centro
La Habana, Cuba

Postscript: We have now a suspect into custody, your bus driver.

"O.K.," I agreed, promising Annie I'd let Bob down gently. Then, trying to appear depressed, I shuffled to my office, where I typed:

Dear Roberto,

My wife and I read *Castanets on the Bus*, and we agree that it [I dug deeply for the right phrase that did not include the words *total dreck*] elicits great promise. I will keep you informed. Meanwhile, please tell your brother to keep the pressure on regarding my precious stoling star. Tell him I am *extremely* happy he has a suspect and that I will do everything I can to make you a famous author. I promise.

Sincerely (I really mean it!),

Gary

P.S. If enough pressure is applied, sooner or later the suspect will confess.

I lobbed Roberto's masterpiece onto my desk, next to my framed eight-by-ten of Charmaine hugging the Reverend Al Sharpton, and admired my nails. Every month or so I'd write Bob another letter to keep his and, especially, his brother's hopes up. He wants to be a writer? Fine. Why should he suffer any less extremely than the rest of us?

Besides, the thought of Capitano Baez pistol-whipping Lopez clack-clacked off the rooftop of my brain like happy little concave shells.

The Power of MasterCard

MY WIFE IS SMARTER, BETTER READ, BETTER EDUCATED, and more cunning than I am. She has a degree in West Indian literature from Northwestern University, whereas I have only a safe-driving certificate from the State of Illinois. She enjoys watching PBS and Discovery; I dig TV Land and the Sci-Fi Channel. She reads Dostoyevsky and Shakespeare on the beach; I tear into Walter Scott's Personality Parade with the gusto of a Chihuahua snarfing a Goober. I was lucky she married me. Just ask her. If I hadn't met her, I would be drinking out of a paper bag and urinating into my shoe.

And it's not only in the intelligence department that we have nothing in common. For example, traveling. She loves visiting exotic locales; I love visiting my couch in good old Mundelein, Illinois. Or temperature. Between taking expensive vacations, she likes the house as hot as Venezuela, whereas I prefer it to have the geothermal properties of Antarctica during that 1950s movie *The Thing*, in which an interplanetary fiend lives in a chunk of glacier until a scientist diddles with the thermostat, causing the ice to melt and releasing the monster, who starts to kill everyone and take over Earth until he gets to Dallas, where the size of the women's hair frightens him into returning to outer space. More on thermostats in a moment, which I promise has to do with traveling.

Annie and I have been married for so many years, I don't remember who was still alive among the original cast of *Saturday Night Live* when we tied the knot. I do recall that I'd wait all week with coiled anticipation for *Fantasy Island*, just to hear that lisping French midget shout, "De plane, boss! De plane!" Or he might have been a dwarf. I never could get those two straight—but I have the same problem with mostaccioli and rigatoni. Even though Annie's family considers the high point of mankind's collective intellectual achievement to be the surprise birthday party—which always features that particular pasta, whichever it is—they also believe, paradoxically, that they are descended from a Germanic super-race of creative geniuses that includes Goethe, Wagner, Luther (not King!), and the guy who invented beer.

Although marrying me was certainly a come-down for her and agonizingly tedious on a daily basis, she has kept the creative side of her brain active by finding new and better ways to torture me without making herself look bad. For instance, after a grueling day trying to convince my father to make me his sole beneficiary, I will be sitting quietly in front of the TV, minding my own business, threatening not a soul, watching great comedies from the 1960s, rubbing my cat's ears, when Annie will appear out of nowhere like an avenging angel and, without a word, turn the room thermostat up ten degrees *and then immediately leave the house.*

Because Babs is curled comfortably on my lap, and Annie knows how much I love my kitty, she can be confident that I will now suffer infected sinuses, cracked and bleeding lips, eyelids that creak along my eyeballs like haunted-house doors, shriveled tongue, desiccated bowels, and peeling brain pan before I'll get up to turn the temperature back down. If, when I see her next, I have the temerity to ask her what the heck she did that for, she'll merely claim that she was trying to make our philodendra more comfortable. Young couples, take note: In any argument in which your spouse has to choose between your welfare and the welfare of a house plant, it's always better to be the plant.

Or the time my best friend, Steve, left a message on our answering machine saying that our old high-school groupie, Bambi, was in town for the day and was *dying* to meet the two of us for dinner, me and Stevie, and that she was very wealthy now, having married and outlived the Oman of Ublabla, and, in appreciation for our having shown her how to play strip poker, wanted to buy us brand new Lexus RX330 SUVs with built-in GPS systems and lifetime supplies of gas, which cost her nothing, since she now owned Ublabla. And—this is the "new and better ways" part—when Annie came home, listened to and erased the message, and "forgot" to write it down because she was preoccupied thinking about starving children in Darfur, and when I pointed out that having specifically asked her if there were any messages for me on the answering machine before she cleared its memory, she could just as easily have said "yes" as "no, not a one, no messages today, not a single one, sorry," and, when it came right down to it, in terms of number of syllables, actually a lot easier, it was clear that I was more concerned about my own hopelessly selfish, probably racist gratification than about pitiful African children.

Or the time she gave my Pee Wee Herman doll to Goodwill without my permission (the disabled). Or when I bought a $350 bottle of Dom Perignon as a future reward to myself for finishing my first novel, and then as I headed into the final chapter, discovered the champagne missing from the liquor cabinet only to learn that she had used it to make mimosas for her ladies' bluebird club (cute little birds).

Or the time she took my cherished car in for an oil change, not to North Pointe Motors, where owner, Tim, has been working on it for years and treats it like his own offspring, but to her cousin Bruno, who needed a few bucks to sort out that parole glitch and who held an Aryan Nation White Power rally on the hood of guess what? "I was just trying to be nice," she snapped, "and, *no*, I have no idea how a swastika got carved into your back seat. It's just leather. It doesn't have *feelings*. In all this time you've never gotten to know *me*."

Many men, especially those who do not admire their wives as much as I, would have at that point, say, killed her. But really, how can you not bow down trembling before talent like that?

Don't get me wrong, I'm not entirely guiltless. For a while I retaliated by secretly wiping the cats' water bowl with Annie's face towel. And once, when she had the stomach flu and ran out of Imodium AD and was writhing around the toilet bowl and groaning for me to please, please, please, *please* rush over to Walgreens for her, I stopped on the way home for a take-home sack of White Castle cheeseburgers, which I know she usually craves but, getting a good whiff, seemed not to thrill her on that particular occasion.

Shrinks call this "passive-aggressive behavior"—a feeble, girly-mannish, and ultimately ineffective way to one-up your wife without making marks and being dragged off to jail in handcuffs—which would be the "aggressive" part of "passive-aggressive." And, let's face it, my fraternity-prankish stunts are pathetically crude sight gags compared to her artistic torture brilliance. By the way, have you ever noticed that shrinks themselves are nuts?

Which brings me to traveling.

Our vacationing trouble began on our Jamaican honeymoon, when I was still too polite to ask her why her suitcase weighed roughly the same as Luciano Pavarotti—the difference being that I did not drag the actual opera star around O'Hare International Airport, from ticket counter to snack bar to coffee shop to bookstore to men's room to cocktail lounge to security check-in to gate and back to cocktail lounge. Nor, in Montego Bay, did I schlep the real, live tenor from baggage carousel to Budget Rent-A-Car to cocktail lounge to gift store to parking lot, into car trunk, repeating the trunk part when said car broke down and we had to wait six hours for Budget to send three ganja-sucking, shirtless Rastas who wanted to know if my wife ever partook of "de tru weed," to which she said, "What the hell—when in Rome…"

The point being, I didn't even get a good aria out of the deal, although I did get a collapsed spinal disk and fourteen choruses of "I Shot the Sheriff," so even twenty years later I can't stop humming the goddamn thing. By the time we got to our hotel room, and I hauled her suitcase onto the bed, and she unpacked her iron, folding ironing board, ghetto-blaster with built-in cassette player, battery-operated TV, hair-curler steaming contraption, electric toothbrush, power nail buffer, kerosene lantern, and Black & Decker variable-speed electric drill with carbide-tipped bit set, I was in too much pain to ask the obvious—so, sorry, I can't honestly tell you why she had packed a drill. She was not then the experienced traveler she is now, so perhaps she was afraid we would get caught in a hurricane and have to personally rebuild our hotel. Or maybe she thought if I broke a tooth on a coconut and needed a root canal, rather than cut her holiday short she would just take care of the matter in our room. I just don't know. It's not like I've ever mentioned it after all these years because the truth is, we really don't talk to each other much. (See "oil change," above.)

Anyhow, the ganja must have made her not only horny but irritable, because when I suggested that my back pain was too severe to let me perform my groomly duty, and that maybe propping myself up and watching the midget (or whatever) shout "De plane, boss! De plane!" might cheer me up, she spun around like the Tasmanian Devil and accused me of being a "Eurocentric, uptight colonial oppressor," and what was the point of a honeymoon in the Caribbean if I didn't want to get stoned and have nonstop sex on the beach? I honestly don't know how the beach got into it at this point, because, for one thing, our room didn't overlook anything remotely resembling sand—I was just starting out then—but rather was on the first floor next to the service driveway and garbage bins, on which having nonstop sex would have been uncomfortable and possibly dangerous.

And so it was that vacationing immediately became a bone of contention between two in-love but mutually spiteful people, in as implausible a marriage as vacationing/bone is an implausible metaphor. But we work with what we have, and as you see, my safe-driving-certificate spite wasn't in the same league as her Northwestern-University spite.

So the following winter when she wanted to cruise up the Amazon (anthropology of Arawaks), and I lobbied instead for the Electronic Games Convention in Las Vegas (Elvis impersonators), we wound up booking Brazil, where I contracted an intestinal parasite the size of her mother's rigatoni (or whatever), after which I spent a quality week at Mayo Clinic in Rochester, Minnesota, eating barium-and-jelly sandwiches and having PVC pipe shoved up my tuchas, while she trudged off to La Samanna Resort in St. Martin—her logic being that since I apparently loved frigid temperatures (see "household thermostat," above), Minnesota in January would probably be a great place to cling to life, should I have an adverse reaction to the anesthetic, while because she appreciated warmth, it was only appropriate that she should spend my intensive care time in the Caribbean.

The year after that, she wanted to take a cruise around the Mediterranean (history and art), but I was more inclined to Oktoberfest in Milwaukee (bratwurst), and our marital compromise got us booked to the Aegean, where I spent the next two weeks being seasick and throwing up into my suitcase, so that I had to buy a whole new wardrobe at our next port of call, which happened to be Kabul, so for the next three days I lay on the Lido Deck wearing a *burkah* and drinking Pepto Bismol through a mosquito screen.

Then it was African photo safari (vanishing species) vs. Wisconsin Dells (Minnetonka moccasins), Eastern Australia (Great Barrier Reef) vs. Dubuque (paddle-wheel boat with slot machines), China (Terra Cotta soldiers) vs. Lake County State Fair (corn dogs), Netherlands (tulip festival) vs. Branson, Missouri (more Elvis impersonators)— the upshot of which was that "we" decided to save the domestic destinations for when we'd be too old to lift ourselves out of a bathtub.

Can you spot the pattern here? Annie, convinced that life is short, likes to experience all things exotic, while I, convinced that sometimes life isn't short enough, enjoy hanging around my creature comforts. I simply do not like any country whose restaurants do not serve tuna melts, where you cannot watch *Wheel of Fortune* in English, and where there are a suspicious lack of stray dogs and cats.

Besides, I detest flying. I once got run over by one of those stupid airport carts that carry old people from one gate to another, and now every time I hear that "*eee-eee-eee*" I freak out and cower behind the check-in counter, which weirds out the check-in ladies, or whatever they're called, although one of the check-in guys did give me his home phone number. And why the hell do old people fly anyhow? Aren't they supposed to be driving around in motor coaches with dachshunds on their laps?

And yet, year after year, Annie managed to drag me from one corner of the Earth to another—and, being a good Republican, I definitely believe the Earth has corners— under the implied threat of taking away everything I own in an ugly divorce, wherein she would reveal in public records that I polish my cat's toenails.

But then, in early 1999, there was a miracle.

One night at dinner Annie passed me the pepper shaker and said, "Let's go to Montserrat. I've got the trip all planned out. It'll be fun. The third week in January when it's the worst weather in Chicago and the best trade winds in the Eastern Caribbean. We'll send our friends postcards to torment them."

"That's Super Bowl week. The only thing they show on Montserrat TV is Queen Elizabeth's coronation—and they think it's happening *now*."

"You can watch the Super Bowl anytime. Tape it for when we get back."

I passed her the salt. "But then I'll already know the score."

"So what're you saying, football is more important than me?"

"The guys expect me, that's all. We missed last year, remember?"

"And nobody died."

"They're going to order in hotdogs and Italian beef." I neglected to mention that Bambi was going to stop by for a little poker.

"And while they're clogging their stupid arteries, you'll be eating fresh grouper with mango chutney. Where it's *warm*."

"But don't you remember, you promised me last year if I—"

"We're going to be dead soon, and we won't have *lived*."

"We're in our forties, and we've been on every continent and every ocean."

"Like you know exactly when we're going to die. Carnak the Magnificent." Which was another of her brilliant tactics because now, of course, it wasn't about the Super Bowl anymore but about my being a control freak.

"Does this have anything to do with my watching Nick at Nite on our honeymoon?"

But there was no point probing, because her having already made up her mind was as immutable as the Great Pyramid of Cheops, and my appealing to her sense of fairness would have been the equivalent of the Egyptian contractor going to Ramses when the project was three-quarters completed and saying, "Problem, boss. The union's calling a strike."

And so it was that, for the umpteenth January in a row, my wife made me face the gloomy prospect of lying under a mosquito net in the middle of nowhere, watching mandibled moths the size of stealth bombers gather on the ceiling waiting for me to go to the bathroom, while my buddies were going to be dealing Bambi deuces from the bottom of the deck and gloriously stuffing their faces with Vienna all-beefs.

I did not want to go. I did not want to go. I plunged into a depressive abyss. I could not sleep. I lost weight (Annie actually put on a few pounds—wanting to fill out the two-piece, I guess). I began to fantasize about my old girlfriends—both of them. It's true, my mother had warned me about getting married before I had had a chance to take a girl out more than twice, after which they always dumped me on the grounds that I was a mama's boy. But I had pointed out to Mommsy that I was almost thirty and therefore perfectly capable of making a marital decision on my own, and, besides, of all three women, Annie was the one who most reminded me of her. But now, in retrospect, those previous two girlfriends were looking pretty attractive, like Ginger and Mary Ann on

Gilligan's Island, although in reality they more resembled Thurston Howell III and, for that matter, Gilligan.

But the more I suggested alternatives—for example, having children—the more Annie dug in, her trump card being that she had studied West Indian literature in college while I was wasting my brain making a living. So what's the point of earning a degree at a great university like Northwestern if you don't derive full value of your tuition by actually seeing the very places you read about? When I pointed out that having wasted my brain working for a living had allowed *me* to pay her tuition while we were not married but only living together, and so technically and probably legally it was *my* money from which we would not be deriving full value by not lollying around gift shops that featured rubber alligators, she merely counterpointed that if having helped further her higher education was making me so intellectually insecure, maybe I should have married a bonobo chimpanzee or a real estate agent. "But O.K.," she said, turning up the thermostat twenty-five degrees, "I can live with that."

So as I faced the fact that, at a minimum, if I somehow managed to avoid joining her in Montserrat—unlikely— I'd have to spend the remainder of my domestic life stuffing ice down my pants, I retreated to my local coffee house,[1] where tossing back one latte after another brought me no relief. They have a chess set there, and I played both sides of games, sometimes white representing Montserrat and black representing Mundelein, Illinois, sometimes the

---

1. Owned by a guy named Mitch, who had the idea of opening a chain of gourmet espresso bars across the country, but whose wife talked him out of it because she was convinced no one would ever pay more than fifty cents for something they could make at home for practically nothing.

other way around, with each move standing for another tactic to get Annie to change her mind, but each and every game ending in Montserrat checkmating Mundelein.

As trip time approached, and the calendar bore down on me, I knew I was beaten. The years in the game had ground me down. It was like when an overweight Mohammad Ali climbed with false bravado into the ring in his pursuit of a fourth title, and everyone felt sad for him and angry because they didn't want to be reminded that their own aging selves were climbing into that ring with him, and they wished time could have stopped with the Rope-a-Dope in Zaire. I was tired, and I didn't want to climb over anymore, I didn't want to go to Montserrat, I wanted to watch the Super Bowl with my pals. So I ordered more lattes and threw them back with abandon and closed the joint up, and drove home through my beloved Mundelein, which seemed even more dark, forlorn, and depressing than usual.

And then I thought—yes, I finally thought it—maybe, just maybe, after all those years of maneuvering and counter-maneuvering and in-out-sideways maneuvering—bobbing, weaving, ducking, jabbing, feinting, blocking, hooking, collapsing in the corner, jumping up when the next round started—the marriage referee had finally counted me out. I just didn't want to answer the bell anymore.

When I crawled into bed that night, Annie was already asleep—dreaming of conch fritters, I suppose. I kissed her on the forehead—maybe my last—and she snorted, "love you" and rolled over. She could afford to love me; our plane tickets had arrived that morning. I lay awake for a while, peering spiritlessly into the darkness, contemplating bachelorhood and loneliness. I am not religious, but I had watched enough of those late-night TV preachers to have more-or-less figured out that if you start mumbling to a Mexican guy named Jesus, who lives in your attic, and you send in a little more money than you can comfortably afford to the address on the screen to prove your sincerity, then this immigrant will sneak down into your bedroom in the middle of the night and kneel next to your bed and threaten your wife with a switchblade in her sleep, which is effective because, like hypnosis, it involves her subconscious, which has historically proven to be more rational than her conscious, and—this is the best part—if you had sent in enough money, your wife's subconscious will do what he says, so it doesn't matter if he's legal or not.

"Who the hell are you talking to?" she grunted from her half-sleep.

"No one."

"Well, quit it," she muttered. "Get to sleep. We need to be rested for the trip." Then she rolled over again, snorfed, and returned to her fritters.

To tell you the truth, I wasn't expecting much, attic-wise. From what I had gathered, the best results came from calling in your credit card number right away into a twenty-four-hour 900 number on the bottom of the screen, rather than depend on the U.S. Postal Service, which, frankly, didn't care whether I went to Montserrat or not and doesn't even know how to spell it. But here I was, totally desperate, soon to be eyeball-to-eyeball with giant moths, my toes about to be nibbled on by lizards, my stomach deprived of any food not containing sand, my teeth brushed with water that, every time you turned on the tap, out would squirt a lamprey eel, and instead of calling in my MasterCard number, here I was, a perfect stranger, silently

asking an illegal immigrant, of all people, to extend me
credit, and, assuming he had a wireless internet connection
up there in the attic with him, he would quickly find out
that my credit score was similar to my ACT score—12, I
think—which is why instead of attending Northwestern
University and reading Russian novels I had to perfect the
phrase, "For fifty cents more you can get a large."

So what I did was, I sneaked out of bed, crept across the
bedroom and stealthily turned on the TV. With the volume
on mute, I found my favorite late-night ministry, the
Heavenly Certificates of Deposit Evangelical, founded by
Reverend Leon Griswold, whose wife, when she caught
him compromising with one of the women who passed
out hymn books, compromised his skull with a combina-
tion Old-New Testament Bible, putting him in a coma for
three years, after which he woke up a blithering idiot and
a great spiritual leader and went on to collect millions with
his rousing sermon, "Leap Out Onto the Highway of
Truth!" before he got run over by a church minibus.

So I memorized the 900 number and gently plucked my
wallet from my pants—always a tricky enterprise when
Annie was in the house—and, leaving the bedroom TV on
so I could see where I was going, tiptoed downstairs to the
kitchen and made the call. The woman on the other end
said my donation was a decent first effort but not quite
enough to earn a free copy of Reverend G's latest CD,
"Drain That Account for the Lord!" and I told her it was a
marital emergency, and she assured me that Jesus was listening. I don't know about him, but my rummaging
around my pants certainly woke Annie, because no sooner
did I hang up the phone than I turned around and there,
standing pretty as you please in the kitchen doorway, was

my fist-pumping, lips-curled-in-satanic-snarling, eyeballs-ablaze-with-searing-yellow-red-flame-licking, jaw-rippling, nostrils-flaring, teeth-clenching wife.

"It was nothing," I said sheepishly, holding up my credit card. "I just wanted to make sure we have enough cash balance to cover rubber alligators."

"You lousy dirty rotten controlling bastard," she growled in the same voice as Linda Blair after Satan set up house in her face. So right away I suspected Jesus was probably a heavier sleeper than the 900-number lady thought.

In truth, I was frightened. The prospect of my wife being possessed by Lucifer—flattering though it was on a certain level—was especially terrifying because it was now too late to request separate beds at the Montserrat Plantation Inn.

Reckoning this irrational fear was the result of a guilty conscience, and further reckoning that I had been caught red-handed, I 'fessed up. "It was only fifty bucks," I whimpered, referring to my donation. "We'll spend more than that on coconut heads."

"Bastard," she repeated. "Crummy, controlling, stinking bastard."

Perhaps she was overdoing it. I looked around, but no one else was there. "Me?"

"I despise you. I *loathe* you."

I peeked over her shoulder. Nope, I was the only loathsome creature in the place. We had not yet gotten cats.

Her head twitched, and for a moment I really did think it was going to spin around on her neck. Her eyes quivered malevolently, she sucked her teeth, snort-sprayed something slick and ominous, hissed, swiveled, strode to the guest bedroom, and locked the door.

It took me a minute to collect my thoughts, such as they are, and then I went back upstairs to see if maybe I had left the toilet seat up again. The instant I entered the room, I spotted the problem.

A "Breaking News" alert was strobing in the corner of the television screen, probably having roused Annie's subconscious from its QVC-One-Time-Offer sleep. It was no longer the preacher on the screen but a newscaster I did not recognize. The volume was already back on. He piped, "We again interrupt our regular programming to bring you this breaking story. We are getting word of a major volcanic eruption on the tiny island of Montserrat in the Eastern Caribbean. We do not yet have specific details or know the full extent of the catastrophe, but a reliable source is quoted as saying that 'a monumental eruption has occurred, a horrible natural disaster.' Facts are sketchy, but apparently there have been many deaths, among which may be European and American tourists. The U.S. State Department has put the region on travel alert, pending evaluation of the eruption's current damage and future danger. Stay tuned to this station for details as they arrive in the newsroom. We now return to our regularly scheduled program…"

I muted the set again, pumped my fist at the ceiling, and whispered, "*Amigo!*"

And then a commercial burst on the screen with the headline, THE POWER OF MASTERCARD.

We never did get to Montserrat, and since the eruption Annie and I have spent our vacations pretty close to

home—Wisconsin Dells, House on the Rock, Galena—
and every once in a while getting on a plane for Vegas. You
can't beat Vegas for a good time, and the restaurants are
great. I dig magic shows and corny lounge acts, and I think
Annie has begun to appreciate them, too.

She was pretty ticked off at me at first. She sulked for a
couple of weeks, as the pyroclastic ash billowed over the
Caribbean, and the pundits were all giving odds on
whether it would lower the temperature of America's eastern seaboard. We were lucky, I guess, not to be living on
the coast. Good old Illinois, nestled right in the country's
womb, cozy and safe next to mother's heartbeat. But as the
volcanic cloud dissipated, Annie's frostiness began to thaw,
and before long we were watching the news cuddled together on the couch.

I'll tell you what I think really happened. I think in spite
of that Northwestern University education, her fancy degree, all those books and intellectual mumbo-jumbo, she
was really kind of scared crapless. Seeing how much clout
I had with the guy in the attic must have given her a lot
to ponder. That I and my Hispanic hit man were perfectly
willing to destroy an entire island, including European and
American tourists, to avoid missing the Super Bowl, gave
her a new kind of…"respect," shall we say? And even if she
had been skeptical at first—what Northwestern University
intellectual wouldn't be?—when that fifty-dollar charge
showed up on our credit card bill, she figured she'd better
start to ratchet down her exotic-holiday wish list. That's
what I think.

One night about a week after the disaster, I came home
early from my monthly poker game (I was going to tell

Annie that I had busted out, but the truth was, I was a little shaky about that poisonous cloud and thought that if she and I were going to get ashed to death, we may as well be together—call me a hopeless romantic). But I couldn't find her anywhere, not in her office, not in the media room, not even in the kitchen scarfing shoestring potatoes. Her car was in the garage, all right, but when I went back into the house and called her, there was no answer. Finally, I drifted upstairs to the master bedroom but stopped cold when I saw that our walk-in closet door, usually closed, was now weirdly half-open. Something didn't seem right, and suddenly that scene in *The Exorcist* in which Father Damien approaches the upstairs bedroom where Beelzebub lies in wait came rushing back in Technicolor. But believing my wife might be in peril—if she wasn't ripe for satanic possession, who was?—I garnered my courage, braced myself, and started to slowly enter the closet.

But the door opened only a few more inches before bumping against something solid. I peeked in and saw that someone had pulled down the trap-door stairs to the attic. I looked up and saw Annie's legs near the top step, her upper half in the attic, sweeping a flashlight beam across cobwebs. I didn't want to announce myself and risk scaring her and having her fall off the ladder, so I quietly backed away and crept downstairs, where, in a little while, once she was down from the trap door, I would pretend to first come home.

"Hey, how's it going?" I would say.

"What're you doing home so early?" she would ask.

"Busted out. Sometimes you win, sometimes you lose. What've you been up to?"

"Nothing. Nothing at all."

And I wouldn't say a word about that wisp of pink insulation in her hair. In a little while, when we would be
canoodling on the couch, I would simply reach over to
give her ear a nibble, nudge the insulation away with my
nose, and surreptitiously tuck it between the sofa cushions
for later disposal.

The Night Ramon Popular Stopped Being a Commie

HE CHANGED HIS NAME TO POPULAR BECAUSE HE thought a good revolutionary should have a charismatic name, like Che Guevara's—although Che's last name had always been Guevara, whereas Ramon's real last name was Blitzstein. He was a plump half-Puerto Rican with Buddy Holly glasses, a Trotsky goatee, and cheeks like scoops of butterscotch ice cream. He was thirty-five years old, and he tried to grow dreadlocks, but he was already balding severely and asymmetrically, so that his hair resembled a nineteenth-century Chinese coolie's more than a twenty-first-century Rastafarian's.

It was funny that he picked the name Popular because among all my friends he was pretty much the least popular. I had introduced him to my poker group, and it was great for about two years, because he lost every single hand except two, and one of those we let him win so he wouldn't get discouraged. But eventually the guys got sick to death of his trying to recruit them into his FALN Puerto Rican separatist movement, the other guys being pretty much successful Jewish lawyers and not giving a shit about Puerto Rico, except insofar as it had good casinos right on the beach. Even Vegas didn't have that, and Atlantic City was for retired bus drivers and other assorted schmendricks like, well, Ramon. So eventually the guys took me aside and asked me not to invite him back, but if he really did want to give away his money every month, could he just give it to me and let me disburse it to the rest of them?

In a way I felt kind of guilty about it, so I tried to be extra nice to him, although he took advantage of it mercilessly, and that's how I found myself one evening sitting at O'Hare, waiting for a plane to San Juan. Here is a tip from a veteran travel writer: If you can avoid it, never fly in or out of San Juan. Puerto Ricans have a special deal with the airlines, wherein—I am not exactly sure how this works legally or biologically—they are allowed to buy one seat for every sixteen of their children, all under the age of five.

Of course sixteen toddlers cannot all fit on one seat, so they let the little brutes run up and down the aisle, screaming almost as loudly as their parents, squirting water pistols at any adult who does not look Hispanic, foraging seat cushions for peanuts, and somehow figuring out a way to lock the bathrooms from the outside. Once, on a flight I took from San Juan to St. Kitts, the plane, suffering from instrument trouble, had to make an emergency landing in Antigua, where mechanics found a Puerto Rican kid wedged behind the altimeter. And no one had reported her missing.

Since the age of eleven, Ramon had been plotting the overthrow of the United States government. At Joyce Kilmer grammar school, he had strutted around the playground wearing Fidelista army fatigues and smoking cigars. At twelve he hijacked a Good Humor truck, drove to the Henry Horner projects, and gave ice cream bars to poor black kids, who, when the treats were depleted, beat the shit out of him and stole his cigars. When he emerged from the police station, he claimed to the *Tribune* reporter that he had been beaten and tortured by the "dirty hegemonic pigs," but later, when writing his "memoirs from prison"—the bathroom of his mother's third floor apartment—he admitted engaging in propagandistic methods to advance the cause of world revolution. "The ends always justify the means," he would say time and again during poker, usually followed by, "A straight beats a flush, right?"

Unlike my poker pals, my fellow professors at the university always sat enraptured by Ramon's tales of Marxist anarchy, our English Department being particularly lousy with Marxist anarchists. I never understood exactly why that is, but my guess is that folks who don't like money usually aren't very good at making any.

In any event, on this occasion, Ramon was going to San Juan to deliver a revised manifesto at a meeting of the Federation of Non-Aligned Developing Socialist Peoples (FONADSP)—of which, to show you how far communists had fallen since Jimmy Carter had warned them that if they did not stop world conquest he would tell their parents, FONADSP had made Ramon its communications director, believing, I suppose, that English teachers were actually knowledgeable about the language. I was joining him in order to lie on a beach, sip rum punches, and critique women's rumps—my wife being home paneling our den. It was eight o'clock, and O'Hare was settling down for the evening. Those electric cars with their stupid warning horns had run over their last bystanders of the day. Hare Krishnas were busy throwing away Canadian coins. Airport security guards, winding down while waiting for their shift to end, had begun X-raying their doughnuts.

I glanced up from my *Big and Buxom Biker Chicks* magazine at Ramon, who was, in his irritating way, clicking his ballpoint pen to the boot-beat of an inner May Day parade. Then, while moving his lips, he began assiduously scribbling in his ever-present spiral notebook. He frowned, bit his lip, puffed his cheek, tugged his goatee, violently crossed something out, jotted again, adjusted his glasses, frowned some more, and burrowed a fingertip into his dreadlock. He looked up at me, his kisser all knotted. I glanced away but was a beat too slow.

"I could use your input, amigo," he said, plaintively.

I shrugged. "You know politics aren't my thing. I don't like touching yucky things like, oh, deadly explosives."

He shrugged back. "You are what you are."

I returned to my biker chicks.

"This is a *creative* writing question," he added.

Everyone's a writer, until it comes time to actually writing.

"I'm sort of on vacation," I said.

"Sooner or later, you'll have to take a stand."

I tapped the sunglasses in my pocket.

"It's a language question."

"You're an English teacher," I reminded him.

"My mother was too busy serving her capitalist masters to help us with our homework. Care to hear more?"

"O.K., what's the question?"

"I can't figure out what to do with the *P* in FONADS*P*. Fonads...*p*. Doesn't exactly glide off the palate, does it? But what's the alternative? Only a vowel will work. But I can't think of any word that starts with a vowel that's as good as *Peoples*." He turned his notebook page and read from his list: "*Anarchists...Organizers...United. United* would work— it's...what do you call it?"

"Adjective."

"But then I'd have to add another word altogether, and it's almost too long already. Come on, you're good at this non-academic stuff."

"How about *Assholes*? That works all the way around, don't you think?"

"Maybe something with an *E*?" He shook his head. "But then it would be FONADSE, which sounds like something you take for gas. A *Y* makes it sound too cutesy, and, let's face it, advocating the armed takeover of the Western Hemisphere is serious business."

I moved to the next row.

Fifteen minutes later, he plopped down next to me, notebook on his lap, beer cup on belly. "So?"

"So what?"

"Did you come up with anything?"

"If I tell you, will you deny knowing me?"

"Deal."

"Drop *Peoples* and tack an *s* on *Socialist*."

He screwed a stare into his notebook. "Lord Jesus. No wonder you make more money than me."

"I make more money than you because I actually know how to read."

"What is that, some kind of class slur?"

I lifted my Diet Coke. "*Viva* affirmative action."

He raised his beer. "Right on, brother."

The check-in agent made an announcement. Our flight was severely oversold.

Ramon grinned satanically. "Corporate greed," he snorted. "That's what I been trying to tell you. You'll see— eventually you'll need us."

"If any passengers are willing to take tomorrow morning's flight," she went on, "AmeriTrop Airlines will be pleased to present you with a $200 voucher, good for any flight at a future date."

"I'm not budging," Ramon huffed. "The bastards got themselves into it, let them work it out."

"The back of the ticket says they can bump us."

He flapped the ticket. "Ideological repressive apparatus! Capitalist oppression!"

"Or," the woman announced, "we have a very limited number of first-class seats still available that we'll offer with our compliments on a first-come, first-serve basis."

I was on my feet.

"Whoa," Ramon called. "Where you going, amigo?"

"Amigo my tuchas. We're flying tonight, and we're flying right."

In a flash, he was at my side at the counter.

I flourished my ticket envelope. "We'll take two first class."

"This is bullshit, man."

"Never mind him," I told her. "We'll take them." I turned to Ramon. "Give me your ticket."

"No way. This is corporate blackmail."

I turned to the agent. "Fine. I'll take one."

"You're selling out, man."

I asked the agent for an aisle seat, if possible, but if she didn't have one, O.K., too.

"You're a pawn, man, a pawn."

"You want to go steerage, that's your business."

"You're the only person I know."

"You've got plenty of other losers back there to chat up revolution."

He handed me his ticket. I relayed it to the agent.

"This just ain't right."

"I won't tell a soul in the English Department."

"Seats 1-A and 1-B. Bulkhead," she declared.

"Bulkhead!"

"Bullshit!"

"Wine and cheese!" I exclaimed.

Ramon's construction boots shuffled behind me on the jetway. I turned around. His head was bowed, his spine curled like a krill. "Grapes in real glass bowls!" I called. "Real silverware! Hurry!"

When we were seated—it really was the bulkhead— Ramon, suspicious, asked, "How is it you know so much about first class?"

"I read about it in an Ayn Rand novel."

"How can you be happy, knowing there are people starving in Chin—" He stopped himself. "Venez—" He faltered again. "New Orleans."

"To tell you the truth, I didn't know about that until you just mentioned it—and, unfortunately for starving people everywhere, I'm already boarded and seated." I squeezed the supple armrests and plumped up a pillow. "Yes, indeedy."

The flight attendant brought over mini-champagnes and bowls of cashews.

"Not your average beer nuts," I observed. "Look, we don't even have to bite open a bag."

"It's obscene."

I licked my fingers. "Nothing but *cashews*. They don't even have those stupid Brazil nuts." I made a stinky face.

The flight attendant asked if she could pour our drinks.

"You bet," I said, pinging my flute.

Ramon leaned over and whispered, "Aren't you ashamed?"

"You bet."

"Would you like me to pour yours, too?" she asked him.

He screwed his eyes up at her, seeing her as if for the first time, seeing that she was Hispanic—an adorable little Latina but without hair on her arms. He spoke to her in Spanish. "*Baranta baranta gallanta baramba rallanta baramba.*"

Her eyes narrowed. She answered, "*Baramba gallanta baranta rallanta gallanta baramba.*" It was at times like this— and, as another example, trying to order a meal in Miami—that I wished I had studied Spanish instead of French. French, like its speakers, isn't useful for much.

She left without pouring Ramon's champagne.

I crunched a cashew. "I'll bet you told her she was an exploited tool of the owner class."

He looked down—guiltily, if I'm not mistaken.

"She told you to go fuck yourself, didn't she?"

He tugged his dewlap.

"Let's have it."

"We might not be getting any more champagne," he muttered. "Or anything else."

I bolted up with both flutes. I cornered her in the galley. She was cute, all right, with a perky nose and eyebrows that were actually separate (one of the differences between AmeriTrop and the "employee-owned" airline). "My friend is a recovering egalitarian," I told her, "but completely harmless. I hope you won't take it out on me." I offered our glassware. "I happen to be crazy about the ruling class. I hope to become one myself. Watch out, little people!"

She filled the glasses with bubbly.

"You'll keep the good times rolling, then"—I glanced at her nametag—"Maria?"

"Hot towels on the way," she assured me. "Meet me at the pass."

I returned to my seat and handed Ramon his champagne.

"What's this?"

"Urine, O.K.? Drink."

He slurped. "Not bad at all."

"Moët, eighty-three."

"The year Reagan invaded Grenada."

She came with steaming towels, rolled up in a basket like terrycloth tamales. With tongs she lifted Ramon's, and it unrolled in a billowy cascade. He stared at it.

"Wash away your sins." I showed him how.

He tried it. "Not bad," he admitted, nodding, dabbing his neck. He sipped a bit more champagne and scarfed a fistful of nuts. "No, not bad at all."

After his second glass of champagne, Ramon put aside his manifesto and picked up *Travel & Leisure* and *The Robb Report*. He flipped the pages with gusto. Maria brought us linen napkins and draped them lovingly over our laps. With regard to Ramon's lap, I use the term loosely.

"I can't believe she doesn't mind being so servile," he whispered.

"She's a handsome woman, don't you think? Smart, too."

"Home girl."

She brought our dinners. Coq au vin, baby boiled potatoes basted in thyme butter, wedge of Camembert, snap peas with walnuts, warm mini-baguette.

"You know you're in first class when the salt packets aren't already cracked open," I explained.

He lifted his flute in Maria's direction. "More champagne, please?"

Dessert came. Crêpe Suzette and chocolate-covered strawberries. Dark, rich, luscious bad boys.

Ramon gobbled two strawberries and burped.

Maria brought us blindfolds. "What's this for?" he stammered.

"They're going to shoot you."

He pried off his boots, put on his headset, slid his blindfold into place, eased back into his rich Corinthian leather, and, if I understood his happy little snorts correctly, snoozed. Among his contented exhalations, he muttered, "Not…a…bad way…to…go."

An hour later, he awoke, ordered a cup of Kahlúa coffee and plate of cookies, and started perusing *Luxury Homes of the Southeast* magazine.

And then it happened.

A woman from coach poked her head through the curtain. As she stepped into first class, towing one of her young beasts, Maria jumped up to block her. "*Gallanta baranta baramba lajolla bazilla.*" The woman kept looking at our toilet door. Maria shook her head. "*Bajilla garanta lajunta tortilla baranta.*" The kid jumped up and down, holding his crotch. "*Baramba ariba ariba tequila bazilla. Ariba, ariba!*"

Maria stepped aside, and the coach woman swept her bambino—or whatever they're called—into our bathroom.

The magazine slipped off Ramon's lap, but he did not pick it up. His gaze was glued to the young mother wedging herself and her offspring into our lavatory. "Are they allowed to do that?" he whispered.

"How the hell do I know? You're the one who speaks Spanish."

"She said their bathrooms were all locked with no one inside, and her son was desperate."

I picked up the magazine for him.

"O.K…I guess," he conceded. "If it doesn't bother *you*." But he couldn't take his eyes off the illuminated OCCUPIED sign on the toilet door. After a minute, he grumbled, "I just think we're entitled to have it available when we need it, that's all." He curled his nose.

"Maybe Maria will fumigate it for you."

"For all of us, really."

"Us?"

He waggled his pudgy fingers. "You know, *first* class."

Economy woman and child eventually scurried back under their rock, but Ramon remained uneasy. He tried reading *Yachts and Yachting* magazine, but his glance kept returning to the lavatory door. He started to wriggle.

"What's the matter?"

"Nothing."

"You have to go to the bathroom?"

"I can wait."

"We won't land for another twenty minutes."

"It's O.K. I can wait."

Later, at our hotel, Ramon called me in my room. "I need to talk."

"I'm getting ready for bed."

"It shouldn't take long."

"I'm naked."

"I'm in crisis."

"I'm trimming my nose hairs, and I need to concentrate."

"Leave the door ajar. I'll slip in."

In a few minutes, I saw him in my bathroom mirror. "Just keep trimming," he said. "I won't distract you." He hunkered down in my bathtub.

I closed the shower curtain and returned to the mirror. "What's on your mind?"

"I've been doing some soul searching," he said through the curtain. "Would you lose respect for me if I asked someone else to deliver my manifesto? Public speaking has never been my big thing anyhow." He sighed.

"Well," I said to the sigh, "the truth is, communism had its day, and we ex-hippies should probably move on with the times. You know, buy jewelry and stuff."

He hesitated. "Did you notice, they have a casino in the lobby?"

"I could teach you to play craps. Blackjack, too."

He cleared his throat. "I was thinking more in terms of…poker."

I scraped aside the curtain. He was resting his chin on his knees. He gazed up at me hopefully. "Poker?" I said.

"I thought maybe if I could play better and agreed not to talk so much about blowing up the International Monetary Fund, that kind of thing…the guys might, you know, be willing to invite me back?"

I put down my tweezers. "Let's go."

"For real? Now?"

I slapped on my shirt and pants, checked my wallet for cash, and we headed for the elevators.

"Are you sure this is right?" he wanted to know. "With people suffering in North Korea? A straight beats a flush, right?"

"Not tonight, amigo."

We got into the elevator, and who should be there? Maria, that's who. All by herself.

"I was a little bored," she said.

"You're in luck," I said. "We're headed for the casino. You know how to play poker?"

Her eyes twinkled. "I'd like to learn." She turned to Ramon. "*Baranta gallanta baramba bajilla godzilla?*"

He smacked his lips. "And blackjack and craps."

"Craps!"

The elevator door opened, and we got off and made a hard right turn, and there before us opened a wonderland of lights twinkling and signs flashing and coins clanking and bells chiming and money flying and people whooping and not starving to death. Ramon's eyes got as big as Sacajawea dollars, and we no sooner stepped into the casino than he put a coin in Big Bertha and started to pull the gigantic lever, when Maria put her hand on his and said, "Better luck this way" in English, and they pulled the handle together and, standing on their tiptoes, watched the reels spin.

Papa's Ghost

I HAD HEARD RUMORS OF HEMINGWAY'S GHOST APPEARING from time to time around Paris, Key West, and even Oak Park, Illinois. For a long time I had the notion of being the first writer to record the great man's specter in Cuba—a kingly phantom on the ramparts of El Morro Castle. As the drawbridge of diplomacy creaked down and I was at last granted permission to travel to the workers' paradise, I made a pilgrimage to the island haunts of my literary idol.

Perhaps there, walking the same cobblestones, gazing at the same sunsets, falling through the same holes in the sidewalk as the master, I would find, to quote Hamlet's father, a "spirit, doomed for a certain term to walk the night."

Hemingway fell in love with Cuba when he first went there during a 1932 fishing trip with his buddy Joe Russell, owner of Sloppy Joe's Bar in Key West, Florida. From Russell's cabin cruiser Hemingway caught nineteen marlin and three sailfish and was, well, hooked.

Two years later he bought his own boat, *Pilar*, and over the next several years popped over to the big island when the spirit moved him, which—given the deteriorating state of his marriage to second wife, Pauline—was more and more frequently. When not on the water, he stayed at the five-story Hotel Ambos Mundos, near Havana harbor.

In 1939, Hemingway's girlfriend, writer Martha Gellhorn, visiting Cuba for the first time, persuaded Hemingway to abandon his bachelor quarters at the hotel and rent a home. She found, and he rented, Finca Vigía— Lookout Farm—fifteen miles from central Havana. In 1940 he divorced Pauline, married Martha, and bought the farm, so to speak.

For the next two decades he lived in the house overlooking the countryside. When he wasn't entertaining celebrities, getting wasted, writing masterpieces and duds, he and his first mate and blood amigo, Gregorio Fuentes, would set sail on his beloved *Pilar* from the nearby fishing village of Cojimar to hunt marlin and, sometimes, submarines. In the mid-1940s, outfitting *Pilar* with armaments, they prowled the Caribbean for German U-boats—which, thankfully for literature—they never encountered.

In 1960 he left Finca Vigía and Cuba for the last time, without packing much. Some offer that as proof that he intended to return when things settled down there, but an Idaho shotgun had other plans.

In Old Havana, swaggering distance from my hotel, El Floridita restaurant pulses like a matador's heartbeat, its huge neon sign visible, I suspect, from Pamplona. It is a clean, though not well-lighted, place, noisy, crowded, and upscale. Despite this being a country where pesos are less valuable than toilet paper, where the one is no doubt used for the other, at Floridita you'll find white-linen table-cloths, candlelight, a menu to rival the trendiest bistros in South Beach, and, as in every other venue in which Hemingway lived, ate, drank, or relieved himself, plenty of photographs of Papa and his entourage: Gary Cooper, Spencer Tracy, Ingrid Bergman. Hemingway, whose atti-tude toward trendy was the same as a hammerhead's toward chum, would not have approved. But then, of course, there are the Floridita's daiquiris: Hem proclaimed them the best in the world. And he was a man who knew his cocktails.

Squeeze past the beautiful *señores* and *señoritas* and belly up to the runway-length mahogany bar where, on its far left, you can catch a glimpse of the great man's favorite stool, enshrined behind a velvet rope. My reaction was, like his favorite cocktail, mixed. On the one hand, my breath came up short as I gazed at the very leather on which the maestro hatched some of his most famous fiction and in-famous grudges. On the other, I felt like telling him to do the world a favor and quit pickling his brain.

Nevertheless, I ordered a daiquiri—reputedly of the same formula as in my hero's time—and braced myself for ghostly nirvana. The drink wasn't bad, but apparitions ev-idently did not get clearance to land. So I ordered another and another still, staring at the master's chair until, amoeba-like, the ivory-colored leather seat doubled and doubled again. If this was where Papa's spirit hung out, the old man's protoplasm must have been fishing, because the only specters that materialized were my own retinal floaters, drifting across my blurry corneas. All right, it was only my first night and it was a big town. Banshees had to be lurking somewhere, and in the meantime I got to take home three nifty El Floridita cocktail stirrers. Perhaps Papa's poltergeist turned in early these days. He was, after all, 102.

The next morning, I ate a hearty breakfast of something-or-other with ham. Then I wound my way through the narrow, cobblestone, canyon-holed streets of Old Havana, past peeing dogs, cigar-smoking *señoras*, and enterprising urchins wanting money for "milk." Once-grand buildings had weathered to the color and consistency of matzo, their arabesque façades dripping with corbels and laundry, their amputated fountains hidden in dreary courtyards pulsing with state-sponsored TV—slouched and faded beauties whose insides were rotting, the way nightly rum eventually rots your guts.

On tapeworm-thin Empedrado Street, I found La Bodeguita del Medio and would have walked right past the narrow storefront had it not been for the clot of fellow pilgrims posing beneath the hand-painted sign for photos of themselves in front of this other famous Hemingway watering hole.

I decided that here, unlike the Floridita fern bar, is where a ghost of true grit would hang out. Here you read the daily specials, which apparently had not changed in years, on a wall, not a damn menu. In this sardine-packed bar, every centimeter of wood is carved with someone's initials or death threat. There is so much beer on the floor, locals come just to preserve their shoe leather. This was, and still is, Hemingway's kind of bar, where each trip to the men's room brings an exponential increase in the risk of emphysema, and the toilet is broken in any case, so you make do with what you have. Yes, del Medio is where I would find my elusive wraith.

"Mojito?" the bartender asked, and before I could answer, he was crushing a mint branch into a glass. Maybe my Banana Republic journalist's vest with pen in every pocket was a giveaway. Never mind, the mojito—rum, lime, sparkling water, lots of sugar, dash of bitters, and aforementioned fresh mint—felt as refreshing as a summer cloudburst. Hemingway is said to have claimed, "My mojito in La Bodeguita, my daiquiri in El Floridita." Judging by the working-class crowd, pestling me against a photograph of Papa and sailfish, this is where I was most likely to find the phantom of the ever-raucous Ernesto.

Unfortunately, though, unlike the earth for Robert Jordan and Maria in *For Whom the Bell Tolls*, otherworldly dimensions did not move for me. Nary a quiver.

All right, it *was* the middle of the day. Metaphysically or not, Hemingway had to write sometime. And I knew exactly where. Off I weaved, several sidewalk-canyons-of-death up the street, to the bustling Ambos Mundos, Papa's home-away-from-Pauline, at the wide, sunny corner of Mercaderes and Obispo.

In the premier corner of this renovated five-story Spanish-colonial beauty, a lovely young docent motioned me into Room 511. The small room was like any hotel overnighter, except that it had once been occupied by the greatest American literary talent of the twentieth century. There were a couple of things you don't normally find in a Motel 6: an Underwood typewriter under glass, a guest book, and obligatory wall photos of Papa and Fidel.

No ghost, though. On his taut-sheeted bed no crater betrayed an invisible man, as it had in the movie starring Claude Raines. At the open window, I gazed over rooftops of the sunlit, shadowed city and squinted at El Morro's tower, trying to imagine Papa's ghost, head in hands, pacing its catwalk. But the only scary vision was a tubby tourist smoking an oversized cigar.

It occurred to me that, as Hemingway had first come to Cuba to escape the tumult of notoriety, perhaps now his incorporeal self had decided to ditch the noise and hubbub of Havana. If so, surely it was to retire in seclusion at his tranquil Finca Vigía. Who's to say phantoms don't appreciate their peace and quiet like the rest of us? Maybe for Hemingway's ghost, it was a weekend-weekday thing.

The next morning dawned gray, dismal, and gloomy, just the right chill, drizzle, and fog to invoke the supernatural. I took a taxi, a 1955 Buick, to Hemingway's hilltop home, fifteen miles from downtown Havana. After paying an admission fee at the gated entrance, my driver chugged up a quarter-mile, tree-lined driveway to let me off at front stairs as wide and white as the writer himself.

At the top of the stairs, a vacuous-eyed young docent welcomed us to Museo Hemingway. She had made her spiel a thousand times, and it showed: *Can't go inside. No flash photographs. Exactly as the writer left the house in 1960. Wrote* For Whom the Bell Tolls, The Old Man and the Sea, *and other famous stories here. Entertained many Hollywood stars and starlets. Recorded his daily weight next to the scale on the bathroom wall.* Pilar *on exhibit around back. When he left he donated the house and boat to the Revolution.*

Say what?

"Donated the house to the People's Revolution," she repeated with a straight face.

The house is a one-story, off-white, stucco villa, not very big—about two-thousand square feet, if you don't count the imposing tower, La Torre Bianca, that Papa's fourth wife, Mary, built for him to write in and that, apparently, he couldn't write in (maybe the view was a distraction).

The claim that the house was exactly the way the Hemingways had left it the day he "donated it to the Revolution" didn't ring entirely true. The whole deal looked pretty staged to me. On his bed lay his fishing cap; shotgun shells stood at attention on his desk; bullfight paintings lined his walls; half-filled Campari bottles decorated nearly every room, as did the heads of the African beasts to whom Papa had just-a-little-too-generously given "the gift of death." (The disembodied trophies had actually been brought in when they turned the house into a museum. I'm guessing a lot of Papa's books—reputedly 9,000—were, too. No one man could read all those, not even in the days before cable TV. You can either entertain Hollywood starlets or you can read, but you cannot, ahem, do both.)

In turn I stared at Hemingway's desk chair, his bed, his sofa, his toilet seat, trying my best to conjure a vaporous, grizzled hulk. But as in downtown Havana, no apparition made itself known.

I followed a slippery, moss-covered, inclined path past the empty swimming pool, past the graves of Hemingway's favorite dogs, to a covered, fenced-off pen, where *Pilar* was waiting stoically for her sailor—or his deathly shadow—to return. A little irritated now at my hero's absence, I bribed the guard to let me climb over the barrier and into Hemingway's fighting chair. I knew Papa wouldn't take kindly to this sacrilege, but I was in a sacrilegious mood. Perhaps he'd reveal himself to box my ears. When the only vision-from-beyond was the guard tucking my dollar into his guayabera, I strode back to the house, stuck my camera through the bathroom window, and took a flash picture of the wall on which Hemingway had recorded his soaring weight.

On my way back to town, I began to wonder if one of the infamous Hemingway grudges included the whole damn city of Havana.

Maybe if Fidel had given the Campari to the peasants, if he had distributed those 9,000 books to libraries across the land, if he had converted Finca Vigía into a neighborhood clinic, it would not have been so bad. But the truth is, although the writer had welcomed the flushing of Batista's filth off the island, Hemingway, son of Oak Park Republicans, was about as keen on communism as a bull is keen on picadors. That his property, which he "donated to the Revolution" in the same sense that a bull donates his ear, would now be laid out like the stucco equivalent of Lenin's corpse; that his beloved boat would be plattered like a stuffed pig for public consumption, must have been galling. That the virile young writer-sportsman so full of optimism in Paris in the 1920s had ended up having his ballooning weight visible to any gawker for the price of admission, must have been, to a wandering but proud soul, insufferable.

As funked out as Hemingway had been after reading the reviews of *Across the River and Into the Trees*, I wasn't expecting much, spook-wise, when, the next day, I visited Cojimar, the home of Papa's friend and *Pilar's* first mate, Gregorio Fuentes—amazingly, still alive at 104. Keen on my new insight, I now had reason to suspect that my hero's ghost no more haunted the fishing village than it had bedeviled Havana. Still, I had come this far...

Gregorio Fuentes came to Cuba at the age of eight when he was orphaned on a ship on which his father, a Spaniard, had been a cook. He first met Hemingway in the early 1930s while escorting *Pilar* through Cojimar harbor in his own boat. The macho writer and the rugged boatman hit it off right away. Hemingway saw something of himself, perhaps, in the Canary Islander's penchant for riding out hurricanes at sea, in his love of cigars, rum, and *señoritas*. Gregorio told his new friend, "Don't worry, whenever you're in Cuba, I'll take care of you." And for the next two decades, he did, accompanying the writer on hundreds of fishing trips as helper and confidant. On land they hung out together in local *tavernas*, exchanging tales of adventure.

Cubans believed—and still do—that in *The Old Man and the Sea* Hemingway pretty much just transcribed one of Gregorio's stories. The writer, always eager to find a slight, must have bristled at this impugning of his creative power. In truth, although Hemingway was dissipated by the mid-1950s, this last great work, which helped him win the Nobel Prize in 1953, could have been written by no genius, pickled or otherwise, but himself. Still, the rumors must have stung.

After Hemingway's suicide in 1961, Fuentes and Cojimar faded into obscurity. Then, in the 1990s, when Americans started returning in dribs and drabs, Papa's favorite Cojimar bar, the seaside La Terraza, spruced itself up, hung plenty of photos of you-know-who, and gave Gregorio his own table (and free meals and rum) from which to regale customers with stories of Hemingway Past.

By then Fuentes was firmly established, by tradition and economic necessity, if not fact, as the certified model for the fictional fisherman, Santiago. To anyone who would listen, it was now Gregorio himself who had gone too far out to sea, Fuentes who had caught the magnificent marlin, Fuentes who had futilely thrashed at the marauding shark. For an extra dollar or two, you could take your picture with the true and authentic old man of the sea.

Even after Gregorio became wheelchair-bound with cancer, cranky and reticent—perhaps it was painful to speak—one family member or another would wheel him into his living room to greet, nod at, shake hands, and take pictures with busloads of tourists. Payment was not required but appreciated. One certainly could be excused for having the feeling that his family, with no argument from the state, was propping the old guy up. It's a wonder they didn't strap a tin cup to the chair.

To a man like Hemingway, after a lifetime of lip service to dignity, there surely would have been something unseemly about his old friend, far beyond a serviceable existence, being wheeled out to meet motor coaches and shake hands for a buck.

As I trudged up a hill to find his house, I wondered how Gregorio could have strayed so far from macho grace. Call me old fashioned, but I believe that after a certain age— say, oh, 101—if you know with reasonable certainty that you're never going to open a topless table-dancing club in Vegas, it is entirely within your rights and possibly your duty to excuse yourself from the next HavanaTur bus, retire to the bedroom, get comfortable, and will your heart to stop.

In searching for his home, I was struck by how the village—a string of cottages hanging like tarnished pearls down the coastal road—had not changed from the old photographs on La Terraza's walls. It was as though someone had turned off a giant switch in 1960 and had yet to flick it back on—a village and city and nation suspended in time, an ancient insect fossilized in amber.

Up a side street I found the small, one-story bungalow with teal trim and clay-tile roof that matched the bartender's description. When I knocked, I half-hoped no one would answer. A moment later, though, a mustachioed man of about forty came to the door.

"I'm a writer," I said, realizing how stupid it sounded.

The door opened wide. "Yes, yes, come in. There have been no visitors for a while. I am his grandson. Wait here. I will bring him."

The living room was clean and uncluttered. On one wall hung a paint-by-numbers-grade painting of Gregorio and Papa. On the floor stood a swordfish sword carved with fishing scenes. The carpeting was sculpted and olive, like my grandmother's in the mid-1960s. All that was missing was a swag lamp.

"Here he is," said my host, as he wheeled in his shrunken grandfather.

It's tempting to say that, like Hemingway's Santiago, "Everything about him was old except his eyes and they were the same color as the sea and were cheerful and undefeated," but it would be a lie.

Gregorio was shriveled and rumpled and dazed and miserable-looking—folds of jaundiced, mottled skin hanging on a bent and brittle frame. His ears, which had not shrunken with the rest of him, drooped like beagle ears. His eyes, nearly shut with skin flaps, were not in the same solar system as cheerful. The back of his hands were black with moles. His head hung at an unnatural angle, much too heavy, not worth the effort. Tumors clung to him like mushrooms to a tree stump, sucking out the last of its nutrients. On the left side of his neck a four-inch bandage partially fell away, revealing a huge bleeding knob.

I wondered what more Gregorio wanted from this earth. Papa would not have thought much of the freak show either.

"I told him you're a writer," the younger man said.

"From...Illinois," I stuttered, not knowing what else to say.

The ancient mariner awoke from his far-off dream. The light caught the slits of his eyes. *"Como?"* he muttered, perking up a little.

"A writer from Illinois," his grandson repeated in Spanish, letting the old man read his lips.

Gregorio raised his head, held it straight, dignity trying to inject itself into his dissolving spine. He held out his hand, and I took it, not prepared for its strength.

Even after his grandson took our picture, the old man would not let go of my hand. His eyes open wide now, the folds of skin willed aside, he gazed into my soul and said, in a deep, strong voice: "Ernesto?"

I glanced at the grandson, who seemed as perplexed as I was.

I turned back to the old man. After another long beat, I whispered, *"Sí.* Ernesto."

"You came back," Gregorio said in faltering English. "You came back," he muttered, releasing my hand and falling once more into his waking dream. But as the younger man wheeled him back into the shadows, Gregorio's smile remained.

When the grandson returned, he seemed a little unsettled. "That was strange, no?" he asked with an embarrassed laugh. "He thought you were someone else." He looked me over. "That has never happened before." Again, a nervous laugh. "You don't resemble *Señor* Hemingway at all."

No, I do not. I am short and thin. I do not fish. I boxed in high school but did not like it much. I get seasick. I've never shot a living thing and hope I never will. Alcohol upsets my stomach, and the only military combat I ever engaged in was on my computer. I've been married only once, to an unfathomable woman who rules my roost, and I never won a single literary prize. My hair is still brown, I've never grown a beard, and none of my prose has ever excited the imagination of my poker group, let alone the Nobel Prize committee.

No, it's not easy to mistake *me* for you-know-who.

But for some strange reason, that withered, tumored, weary-beyond-endurance old man, who even at the impossible age of 104 was still waiting for God-knows-what to call it a day, thought he saw something in a certain visitor, possibly his last on earth, that Cojimar afternoon, something that brightened him for a moment—a phantom, a ghost, a memory—before he lapsed again into his dream.

A clear case of mistaken identity.

The next morning the old man did not wake up. But he waited a few more days to die. Perhaps he spent that time, impenetrable to visitors, savoring the memory of the reunion for which he had waited so long.

We writers are an insecure lot, searching for validation where we can, roaming ramparts for the spirits of dead idols who might assure us that we're not fakes. So it's tempting for me to make something profound and self-assuring out of the old fisherman mistaking me for the greatest writer of the twentieth century.

But the truest sentence I can write is that one old man with longevity in his veins lived to the point of dementia. He might well have mistaken a broom for Hemingway, or me for a broom. He would have died on that day whether I was in Cojimar, Cuba, or Mundelein, Illinois.

When someone once asked Papa what Pauline died of, he reputedly said, "She just died, that's all, like everyone else, and now she's dead." No pussyfooting with profundity in this joint, pal.

Still, as I look over the photos of my pilgrimage—me in *Pilar*'s fighting chair, me sitting at Papa's table at La Terraza, me crouching next to Hemingway's old man as he breathed his final breaths—it's easy to forget, for a little while at least, that there are no such things as ghosts.

A Bug in My Eye

MY WIFE AND I VACATION AT A BED-AND-BREAKFAST inn, Hermitage Plantation, on the Caribbean island of Nevis. Columbus discovered this tiny, gumdrop paradise in 1493 and quickly named it *Nieves,* the Spanish word for *departure tax.* At the time, the island was inhabited by 500 Arawak Indian peoples and 16 Jewish peoples, whose ancient synagogue you can still visit for normally five dollars but for you, three-fifty. Columbus immediately recognized the potential of these Jewish peoples as hardy field slaves, which is why Queen Isabella personally flogged him in the Cádiz public square.

If you look at a map, you will see that the island chain known as the Caribbean, or, to confuse you, the West Indies, lies between Florida and South America and resembles a string of gems or possibly drool. Some of the islands run east-west and some north-south. This geological anomaly was designed by the American Association of Travel Agents in order to give their clients variety. In Caribbean travel, variety is crucial. For example, some people prefer Carib beer, some Red Stripe. I happen to like Carib because it once prevented me from having an eye transplant.

Which brings me back to the Hermitage Plantation. Nestled into the edge of a lush rainforest at the hem of an ancient volcano, the inn consists of a 250-year-old restored great house and fifteen traditional Nevis-style gingerbread cottages. During the day you sit on your private veranda measuring the hues of the sea and listening to coconuts falling on stray dogs. If you are lucky, a sugar apple will drop onto your roof, followed by monkeys' footsteps, followed by the sound of them attacking one another.

My wife likes to visit the Hermitage in the spring, when butterflies and hummingbirds and finches are the most plentiful. But I prefer to go down in late December, in order to avoid Christmas in the States. I do not like Christmas, since it involves exchanging presents with people who would prefer to see me dead, and it puts a lot of money in the U.S. Postal Service's coffers, which it needs in order to pay higher salaries to mail carriers so they can buy more powerful automatic weapons.

Christmastime at the Hermitage is usually quiet. The owners, a Falstaffian horse breeder and his efficient wife, whose smile is as big as a soup tureen, respect their guests' right not to have the holidays shoved down their $450-per-night throats. At the Hermitage you will find no tinsel or candy canes strung around doorways, no Christmas music pinging acid-like on your skull. The only time you'll even remember it's December is when renegade gangs of local school children assemble on the dining terrace to sing carols. The owners probably do not like this intrusion on digestion any more than I do, but they know what will happen to their water supply if they don't cooperate.

In any event, you can imagine my panic when, last December, I had just finished a lobster salad sandwich on the great-house patio and was ambling toward the library to see if I could find a copy of my last novel when, turning the corner, I spotted, crouching between bookshelves as if coiled to strike, an eight-foot-tall fake evergreen tree, replete with gold garland, shiny blue balls, and tiny, malevolent silver cherubs. My stupefied gaze fell to the base of the tree, laden with colorful foil-wrapped "presents"—although I suspect they were really empty boxes of corn flakes and Uncle Ben's Converted Rice, wrapped to look like they contained clothing purchased at Miss Henny's Hut of Good Deels.

I reeled, clutching my chest, as if NASDAQ had just dropped another 300 points. I blinked at the phony spruce in all its looming horror. Would I never again be able to make my way to the Hermitage's extensive collection of *Popular Mechanics* without confronting this bejeweled Jezebel?

I had to get to the bottom of this betrayal. I sought out Shaba the bartender, a paradigm of good sense and sympathy.

"We put it in the least conspicuous corner of the house," he explained. "Not many people read anymore."

I staggered away, closing my eyes as I passed the library, and collided with the piano.

"Why are you limping?" Annie asked when I returned to our cottage. She was swinging in the veranda hammock.

"They have a Christmas tree! Silver angels, too!"

Her head drooped to her right. "Take a jog. Work off the angst."

"I don't want to jog. I like my angst. I want to go home."

"Christmas with my family, dear?"

"Point taken. I'm going for a jog."

She pushed off, foot to railing, replenishing her swing. It should be said—and I say this with great affection—that the moment Annie's lungs take their first breath of Caribbean air, her normally well-grooved brain turns to smooth conch meat.

I threw on my running duds and sprinted up a steep mountain path, hoping I would fall, roll back to the main house, crash through the library wall, and crush the fake presents. But, as luck would have it, the only untoward event was a stinging insect flying into my left eye and doing what nature put it on earth to do. It felt like a microscopic Christmas tree angel was pouring molten silver into my tear duct. I bent over, covered my eye, and yowled. When I let go of my face, the left half of Nevis appeared to be under water and growing dim. Terrified, I ran back to our cottage.

"Short run," Annie observed.

"A bug flew into my eye," I cried. "I'm dying in a foreign country. Do you have any idea how much it'll cost to ship my body back home?"

That got her out of the hammock. Another endearing fact about my wife: when it came time to purchase my life insurance, she found a policy whose death benefit was indexed to the increased costs of vacations. Incidental expenses—say, for my funeral—she would have to pay for out of her piña colada fund.

"Let me look," she said, eyeballing my eyeball.

"I don't want to die in the tropics," I mewled, recalling the time I sent a souvenir rum cake to my brother in Chicago, and it arrived eighteen months later as an ant farm.

"Maybe we should go to the clinic."

I focused my good eye accusingly on her kisser. The clinic? So, she was trying to kill me after all. Me, the man who still takes messages from her former boyfriends—none of whom rubbed her bunions, I'm guessing.

"The clinic?" I asked, suspiciously.

"I'll be with you the whole time."

On Nevis there is a persistent rumor regarding High Ground Clinic: if you have an ailment of any organ or appendage that comes in pairs, kiss one of them goodbye—not necessarily the bad one. So I immediately assumed they would remove my eye, owing to its being mildly pink, and replace it with whatever they had conveniently available—which at this time of year happened to be a Christmas ornament. A shiny blue ball ornament with *NOEL* written in gold sprinkles, so that for the rest of my life the word would appear backward on the left half of whatever I was reading.

"Forget it," I said, flatly. "I want to die with secular corneas. Shaba will know what to do."

We made our way back to the main house. I am not sure I have adequately described the salubrious effects of the Hermitage bar, particularly when Shaba is at its helm. If there is a God, I imagine he tends a big Hermitage bar in the sky and looks exactly like Shaba: short, stout, with a head the color and texture but not the size of a coffee bean. Supremely wise, eternally comforting, Shaba is the spiritual soul of the Hermitage. In a phrase, he knows everything. And on this, the occasion of my being on the verge of having an eye replaced with a hollow glass ball casting *LEON* on my bedroom ceiling each morning like those time-projecting clocks from Sharper Image, Shaba did not disappoint.

"A bug flew into my eye while I was jogging," I whined, leaning over the counter so he could get a good look. "What should I do?"

Shaba did not hesitate. His mind being filled with an encyclopedic knowledge of modern and folk remedies, Western, Oriental, USDA approved, herbal, homeopathic, experimental, and preventive, he spat out the answer without even glancing at my swollen mug: "Don't jog."

Among other things, Shaba is a man of few words. The laconic efficiency of a monk.

I gazed at Annie with satisfaction. *Aha!* my glare declared. *Shaba has said nothing about a clinic!*

"In the meantime?" she asked the bartender.

"Close your good eye," the maestro told me.

I complied.

He plopped a bottle onto the bar top. "What color?"

"Brown."

"Label?"

I squinted. "Yellow circle, blue letters."

"Brewed in?"

I squinted harder. "St. Kitts."

He spun the bottle around and pointed to small letters. "Serve at what temperature?"

I screwed my damaged eye more or less into focus and concentrated. "Forty-five to fifty degrees Fahrenheit."

He opened the bottle and poured me a drink. "You'll be fine in an hour. Good as new, better than ever."

And so I was. Fine and drunk on life. Annie was swinging in her hammock again reading her book on rainforest poisons. NASDAQ was down only 5 percent on the day. Midnight the cat was sharpening his claws on my nipples. Life was good.

On my way out of the bar, I decided to take a detour to the library. There, I closed my good eye and with the stung one tried to focus on the Christmas tree. It wriggled and swam, but I could definitely make out its shape.

It was definitely a tree. I could even see its ornaments and the wrapped boxes at its base. I could make out individual shapes and sizes. The fact that the presents were all fake did not matter. I could see them; my vision was coming back. As Shaba had said: good as new, better than ever.

I went back to our cottage and told Annie we should consider making a Christmas donation to High Ground Clinic. It must have been the liquor talking. She thought I was having sunstroke and, apparently believing I would collapse before revealing the location of my emergency $100 bill, she lurched at me and got all twisted up in the hammock, and I had to call Shaba and Nelva the maid to help untangle her in time for dinner.

Weed Killer

I WAS IN BARBADOS WRITING AN ARTICLE ABOUT horseracing for a British travel magazine, when the magazine's cunningly parsimonious manager, a Trinidadian-Brit named Vee Kumar, offered me a job writing an article about Caribbean cockfighting. This was before the internet tech help lines, so unskilled East Indians could only get jobs either as indentured servants or editors. The article would pay pretty well—more than twice his usual miserly fee—but since Kumar had no intention of paying me to traipse all over the West Indies, I'd have to research the cockfight piece in the same trip with the horserace piece, and since Barbados, the most British and therefore the most civilized of the islands, didn't participate in such barbarity as chicken fighting, could I, you know, just pop over to Grenada for a little look-see? Lots of barbarity there, Vee knew for a fact, and, by the by, he happened to know someone.

To the average sun-lusting planter's punch jockey, this might have seemed like a great gig, except that it was in September 1983, when Grenada was in the midst of a vicious political power struggle that had all the earmarks of impending bloodshed. The deputy prime minister, a Marxist revolutionary and best friends with Fidel Castro, was threatening to publicly eviscerate the real prime minister, a reformed socialist who was sick and tired of their Cuban advisors fornicating with local livestock. Literal and figurative red flags were all over the place, and I may have been a hungry writer, but I was not stupid.

True, I am an ardent anticommunist but only as long as it does not involve actual bullets. For example, the Vietnam war, against which I had absolutely no philosophical aversion until the selective service called my number, at which time I raced down to Big Dick's Hot Dog and Donut Ranch and roped me enough kosher dogs and Bismarcks to induce a heart murmur loud enough to assure me a medical deferment at a time when Uncle Sam was drafting guys who slept with dolls—in iron lungs. The downside was that I had to listen all day to Big Dick, and there were many moments when I thought it might be better to be impaled on a *punji* stick.

As anyone who grew up in Skokie, Illinois in the 1960s knows, Big Dick's favorite pastime—besides making doughnuts—was regaling his customers with his favorite World War II personal atrocities. Some veterans shunned talking about their war transgressions, but not Big Dick. "After we shot Krauts," he would thunder over his giant Mixmaster, "we liked watching rats eat their gonads." In the Battle of the Bulge, Big Dick got his right hand shot, so now it dangled atrophied and useless. He was a hulking man with a voice like a bazooka, but his right hand was the size of a baby's. You could tell he had been right-handed before his war injury by the shape of his doughnuts. Even in 1968, theoretically circular pastries came out looking like the Belgium border after the Nazis encroached, dug in, retreated, made a surprise counteroffensive, were beaten back, regrouped, attacked the allied flanks, surrounded and nearly pinched off two battalions, but were counter-counter-maneuvered and decimated by George Patton. Big Dick's signature treat, the French doughnut, looked more like occupied Poland.

The point being, I'm as patriotic as the next guy, as long as it doesn't result in actual, say, inconvenience. Which is why, getting back to cockfighting, I wasn't totally excited about popping over to Grenada for a look-see. On the other hand, my cunningly parsimonious editor did suggest that if I didn't write the bird article, my horse article would wind up in a glue factory in New Delhi, along with my check. But he assured me that should I get stuck in Grenada while it exploded in counterrevolution, I could probably subsist indefinitely on bananas and coconuts, providing I could forage under the cover of darkness. "That should be no problem for you, I suppose," he ventured. "You did serve in Vietnam, I presume."

Which is why I soon found myself checking into the Sunrise Guest House overlooking the bay on the outskirts of St. George's, Grenada's picturesque capital. Unfortunately, the seaside city did not lately feel so picturesque. Since the Cubans had come—to train Grenada's military and build a new airport, which, to American eyes at least, seemed more of a size to accommodate long-range bombers and troop-transport planes than tourist puddle-jumpers—the town was deathly quiet. Cruise ships, normally two and three a day docking at St. George's colorful quay, had, for the past six months, given the island a wide berth. Spider webs laced sagging spice stands. Fruits and vegetables rotted in stalls. Souvenir shops were locked and abandoned, their owners hunkering down at home or in church, girding for the worst.

Sunrise's owner, Mrs. Wilsmith, an elderly, genteel black woman as fragile as a finch, insisted on carrying my bag to my room, dying sunlight tingeing her gray hair red. I followed her over a narrow path of coral stones, winding through a tangle of tropical weeds. When I tripped over a bramble, she winced. "We had to let Alford go," she apologized. "Couldn't pay him anymore. Things have been difficult, you see."

"Alford?"

"Our gardener. Crazy Bones, but I've known him since he was a boy, before they called him that dreadful name."

"He's the guy Vee wants me to see about cockfighting."

"Quite right. Mr. Kumar is one of our favorite guests. He certainly can hold his liquor. "

"Especially when someone else is buying."

She hefted my bag onto the bed. "Alford will be very glad he remembered." I offered her a dollar, but she coughed with gentle indignity. "I'll ring him up for you." She stopped at the door and turned. She whispered, "You might want to offer *him* a little something, if you find him particularly helpful. Are you a communist?"

I made a stinky-face.

"Money is a nice thing sometimes, don't you think? What time would you like your tea in the morning?"

"I'm exhausted. Better make it eight-thirty."

She whispered, "I'll call Alford. He hasn't always been crazy."

I woke at seven to the metallic-sweet smell of weed killer. I knew the faint aroma well, and at first I thought it was the beginning of a nightmare. I recognized the smell because for the previous six springs my wife had made me spray the toxin on anything in her garden that was not directly related to purple cone flowers and black-eyed Susans. My wife loves English gardens, particularly those with thorns that impale husbands' ankles, as if the Revolutionary War was our fault.

Sunlight sliced through my shutters and fell diagonally across my bed. Some guy was whispering just outside the window. I strained to hear. Silence. Maybe I really had been dreaming. I tiptoed out of bed and peeked out a slat. Sunshine glinted off a sweating bald spot, oblong as a racetrack and black as lava. Alford was scolding the weeds. "You vexin' Mrs. Wilsmith. You boys have a party when Bones not around, eh?"

My first thought was to bring old Crazy Bones home with me, to prove to my wife what happens to your cerebral cortex when you inhale too much Weed-B-Gone. But then I asked myself, really, what was her incentive for keeping me sane anyhow? I opened the shutters and stuck my head out the window, to see if Crazy Bones was talking to someone just outside of my line of sight. Nope.

"You up now?" he said, gazing at me from between weeds, eyes wide and asymmetrical. "I comin' by de door."

"Give me a minute to get dressed. Maybe you can find Mrs. Wilsmith and ask her to get my tea early."

"Tea comin'," he assured me, then ran toward the reception area.

Ten minutes later, Mrs. Wilsmith was at my door with a tray, Crazy Bones right behind, drying his hands on his pants. "What do you know?" she trilled, "As luck would have it, Alford happens to have a little time on his hands this morning. Lucky for us, I should say."

Crazy Bones filled the doorway. He was a marionette without strings—long-limbed, angular, twitchy. He jerked into the room. His eyes were soft and kind, but they didn't shine like Mrs. Wilsmith's. His left lid drooped halfway. He had very white buck teeth. In Britain they would have called him a dolt, so I instantly understood why Vee Kumar, who knew cheap, gullible labor when he saw it, would have befriended him.

"I'll leave you two gentlemen to your business," Mrs. Wilsmith said with a tiny bow. She had put two cups and saucers and a plate of sugar cookies on the tray. "Don't worry," she assured me, "Alford washed his hands with soap and hot water right in front of me." She flashed him a good-boy smile and padded out.

I motioned for CB to sit. He eyed his tea and cookies, and it took me a minute to figure out he was waiting for me to go first. When I did, he dug in.

"So," he said, slurping and chomping, "you a friend of Mr. Kumar."

"He said you know something about cockfighting."

He stopped gnawing.

"I'm writing an article for his magazine," I explained. I opened my notebook. "I thought you could give me a few details."

Silence.

I clicked my pen a few times. Perhaps one of us, or Vee, had misunderstood. "Well," I said, "if this isn't a good time for you, maybe—"

"You can come tonight? To see a match?"

"A real cockfight? In person?"

"Me own bird fightin' tonight. I can get you at six-thirty."

Good old colonial service at its best! I lifted my cup in a toast. "Here's to Mr. Kumar."

He picked me up after dinner. He wore shabby sandals, tan trousers, crumpled but clean, and a tight, greenish-brown knit shirt that made him resemble a kiwi.

"Someone I want you to meet," he said.

Oh, great. It wasn't bad enough going off at night with a weed-talking cretin referred by an editor who, if he hadn't been an editor, would have been a Gypsy pick-pocket—but now it turned out he had an accomplice. I hadn't the slightest doubt that they intended to chop me and sell my meat as chicken nuggets, the profits finding their way to my editor's Bombay bank account.

"Ivan de Terrible," Bones said, opening his car door for me to get a good look. In a cage on the back seat, his fighting rooster clucked hello.

"Can I take his picture? For my article?"

"Yes, man. Ivan would like it fine."

In Alford's creaky and rust-devoured Daihatsu, we drove up Grenada's rainforest spine. We didn't talk much, because driving through a Caribbean jungle at night is a place for human silence and feeling insignificant. Anyhow, he was quiet and preoccupied, deep into some inner world, and, as in the rainforest itself, I felt like an intruder. I hoped he was concentrating on the so-called road. Every few minutes he would wake up out of his dream to ask me if I had ever been to Grenada. Three times he asked. Twice he said that Kumar was a good man. Then, chewing his lip and clutching the wheel, he fell back into his private abyss.

With my window rolled halfway down I listened to the hoarse calls of nightjars, the rhythmic squeaking of tree frogs—ghost children riding rusty swings—the clacking of insects feeding on one another, and the soft whoops of vervet monkeys reassuring themselves against the terrors of night. And, always, the Daihatsu's springs creaking from deep pain.

Ivan scratched his feet on the slats of his cage, eager, apparently, to face his enemy. The moon had not yet risen, so even in the rare patches of sky, there was no light to relieve the claustrophobia—only the bounce-back of the Daihatsu's anemic and lopsided headlights and the faint dashboard glow that Bones's flesh devoured.

At a mountainside spigot, he stopped, took a plastic Hinckley and Schmitt jug from his trunk, and, at the grainy edge of a headlight, filled it under the squeaking faucet. The water shone like liquid silver. He stuck his head under the spigot and cooled whatever worries were burning his brain. Then he took another jug, unlabeled this time, from his trunk and put it on the rear floor and uncapped it. I recognized the smell.

He scooped out Ivan and put him on the seat. The rooster remained docile and trusting. Bones tilted the bottle until a little liquid filled his palm. He rubbed his hands together and glazed Ivan's head and ruff, avoiding the bird's eyes. He put the bottle back in his trunk, unwrapped a bar of soap from tinfoil, washed his hands under the standpipe, shook them off, and got back into the car. From his glove compartment he took a bottle of Old Spice aftershave and doused his palms. I asked no questions, and he didn't volunteer any answers.

We reached a mountain settlement crudely stitched by a cratered dirt road. Between banana trees, the sea stretched black and bottomless. He parked his car under a bearded fig, behind a row of other cars, in front of a listing shack on cinder-block footings. "Carlysle's house," he said.

He nodded to three men leaning against a fender, drinking from plastic cups.

"Bones, man. Can't start without you. Got Ivan?" They eyed me more with curiosity than suspicion, then immediately fixed on Alford's bird. One of the men ran his finger across the cage's wire-mesh door. Ivan puffed up, thrust out his chest, flung his head back, and crowed. Some cocks answered from Carlysle's yard, and Ivan flapped his wings furiously against his cage.

"He look O.K."

"Fine, fine," Bones assured them.

He brought Ivan to the backyard. It was noisy and animated, filled with tobacco smoke, the sound of clinking bottles, and people shouting over a tape player. There were about fifty Grenadians. He said he recognized a couple of girls from St. George's. Most of the spectators were men, though. They shouted hello and came over to shake his hand, pat his back, and issue encouragement. He introduced me. As Bones's friend, I was all right.

There was a stevedore with a nutmeg-sized forehead tumor, and Cutter Laidlow, a taxi driver whose wife ran a spice shop on the quay. There was Crawfish, a union organizer, and Tulia, a prostitute from Grand Anse. Holding a cigarette and plastic cup in one hand and nothing in the other, she cha-cha-ed over and kissed our cheeks. A priest from Grenville, Père Marcel, eyed me like an iguana. I made the mistake of saying a few words in French, and he was on me like slime. I couldn't shake him, but since Bones, now more distracted than ever, was proving to be a scant source of information, the little Holy Roller came in handy.

Both Father Marcel and Bones knew the Cubans, who worked on the new airport construction at Port Salines. They knew their foreman, Hernandez, and didn't like him. It wasn't bad enough that his Cuban cocks had beaten all the local birds. The foreman, said Marcel, was arrogant and insulting. When there were no worthy contenders left, he insisted on fighting the biggest rooster in Grenada. The locals were going to bet on Ivan, even if he was a huge underdog—a matter of national pride.

Carlysle's wife, Eulalie, her head wrapped Martiniquan style, stood next to a wobbly Formica table, overseeing a Maxwell House can overflowing with U.S. and E.C. dollar bills. On the table were two half-gallon bottles of Mount Gay and Pusser's rum, three listing stacks of plastic cups, a liter bottle of Canfield's seltzer, a dusty box of M&Ms, and a box of White Owl cigars. On the ground behind the table hunkered a case of Carib beer, a case of Coke, and a galvanized tub of mostly melted ice.

I ordered a rum-and-Coke for Alford, Carib beers for me and Father Marcel, and plucked out a cigar. "Where Carlysle?" Bones asked Eulalie. She nodded at the house, where her husband stood on the inside of a Dutch door, handing Crawfish back a cock he had just weighed. The union agent shrank back into the shadows.

Carlysle had built a more-or-less round cockfighting pit out of stakes and chicken wire. The floor was honey-colored sand from Petit Caillou Cove, which, Marcel claimed, absorbed blood better than sand from other beaches. A string of light bulbs drooping between palm trees cast hangman shadows over the pit.

When Carlysle saw us, he came out. "You the first fight, Bones," he said. "Get going."

In nasally English—he quickly figured out I'm a francophony—Marcel explained that normally a main event would have been saved for well into the night's program, but the Cubano had boasted that even a six-and-a-half-pound Grenadian cock was not worthy of being considered a main event against his three-pound, one-eyed Spanish bankiva, El Diablo. Apparently the construction foreman wanted to take the Grenadians' money before they had a chance to spend it all on Eulalie's M&Ms.

Carlysle's eyes darted around the yard. Something was going on. Marcel claimed he didn't know what.

Hernandez was sitting on a folding chair on the other side of the pit, pretending not to notice us. Bones went to the Cuban and offered him a look at Ivan.

"What the hell for?" the construction foreman chuffed. He was wearing new jeans tucked into ostrich cowboy boots, a green-and-yellow floral shirt with papers sticking out of his pocket, and a straw hat with a sprig of cock feathers. He had a ferret face the color of weak tea, and although he was skinny on top, his belly stuck out, the rhinestones on his belt buckle catching the light. He offered us Cohibas, but we declined. Hernandez grunted, insulted. He unwrapped one for himself, lit a U.S. twenty-dollar bill, and, with exaggerated suckings, started the cigar with the flame.

His Cuban associates roared with laughter, apparently restoring some of the foreman's pride.

"I'm surprised you showed up with that goose," he said, flicking his ashes at Ivan and spitting on the ground.

"I hear Cuban cocks small and give up too soon," Bones said, sounding rehearsed. Still, surprised at his temerity, I gave the weed-talker a closer look.

Hernandez's eyes narrowed. His comrades stopped laughing. The foreman blew smoke at Ivan's cage and sneered, "Make it three to one, *pendejo*."

"I scrape up another thousand."

"*Bueno.* Your three to my nine. *Bueno.*"

Next to Hernandez, at the cock display area, twenty cages were stacked into a pyramid. Half-cut plastic milk-jug water bowls, resembling human skulls, poked through the cages. A few spectators were looking over the combatants, filliping the mesh, goading the roosters. Furiously the birds scratched the floors of their cages, thrust out their chests, flung their heads back, flapped their wings, and crowed. Apparently the bettors either liked a bird's fighting spirit or they didn't. If, on prodding, a rooster lunged at a finger or threw himself against the mesh to get at a neighboring bird, it roused a hefty bet.

It was almost nine. Bets and counterbets flew across the yard. Father Marcel offered thirty dollars on Ivan. A Cuban answered with a wad of American bills on El Diablo. The cocks were pecking hard at their cages and crowing.

On one table, Diablo's handler, a runt named Pescador, finished attaching the bankiva's spurs. When Pescador strutted to the ring, the spectators became subdued. The bird panned the crowd with his dark, glinting eye. He had a small head, sinewy white legs, a rust-red torso that looked like a mortar shell, and a brilliant yellow ruff. His tail had been trimmed, making him look even smaller. Pescador set him down to get him warmed up and impress the Grenadians. Diablo swaggered around the perimeter, his steel spurs trailing like comets, his ruff distending lion-like. There was something mystical about him, something foreboding. He was a bankiva cock—pure Spanish—and, said Marcel, cruelty was in his blood.

The priest, standing close to me and reeking of garlic, provided a running commentary. Bones went to the opposite table to fit Ivan. He unzipped a Nike bag, spread out his paraphernalia, and got to work. He wrapped two cotton balls around Ivan's right leg, then slipped an alloy shoe over the sawed stump of natural spur. Next he fitted a two-and-a-half-inch curved saber into the slot in the shoe. Over this he fixed a square of chamois and a leather gaiter. With an eighteen-inch length of gaff string, he bound Ivan's armory to his foot, checking and rechecking the angle of the gaff with every loop of thread. He repeated the process on Ivan's left foot, kneeling on the floor to make sure the angles of the swords matched. Ivan's long yellow legs shone from the warm rum-and-herbal massages Bones had given him over the past five weeks, since he had been laid off from Sunrise Guest House. He had thinned out Ivan's back and vent feathers so he wouldn't overheat, and his comb was short and erect. Ivan was an older bird, and he had not fought in over a year, the priest explained. "But he stands tall and dignified, *n'est-ce pas?*"

When Alford carried Ivan to the pit, the crowd momentarily hushed, then broke out into wild cheering and a frenzy of bets.

Pescador scooped up El Diablo and left the ring while Bones exercised Ivan.

Poised, neck extended, back taut, the local rooster strode back and forth in the ring, his magnificent tail resembling a Mayan headdress. But he was a huge, ambling bird, and there was something slightly comical about his gait. Some of the Grenadians winced.

Ivan the Terrible, though, obviously remembered what it was to be a fighting cock. His eyes shone, taking in all around him, searching for an antagonist. He spotted El Diablo in Pescador's arms, struggling to get at him. Ivan stood motionless—noble, thoughtful, sedate. The crowd did not seem to like the fact that their bird did not act perturbed.

Carlysle stepped into the pit and made his announcement. He motioned for the handlers to approach. He stuck his nose into each bird's feathers, smelling for poison. Some were almost impossible to detect, but Carlysle, Marcel swore, had an experienced nose. The host gestured for the men to bill their birds.

Holding their roosters like bowling balls, they stepped to the near score lines—poker chips nailed into the ground two feet apart. They rocked the cocks back and forth so the birds could get a good look at each other.

El Diablo's neck stretched and writhed snakelike. His eye flashed and his beak snapped malevolently. But Ivan the Terrible was unaroused. Bones jostled him to get him to show some fighting spirit, but the Grenadian bird remained placid. Perhaps something about Diablo's missing eye threw him off.

Suddenly El Diablo sprang out, grabbed Ivan's comb, and shook the bigger rooster's head like a scrap of garbage. Ivan squawked in pain, but Diablo held on viciously until Pescador jerked him away. Ivan was no longer apathetic. He became frantic with rage, snapping futilely at Diablo, and Bones had trouble holding him. The crowd went wild. The odds narrowed.

"Pit your cocks," Carlysle instructed.

The men walked to the far score lines—eight feet apart—put their roosters on the sand, and quickly stepped back. Despite their murderous hatred for each other, the birds did not attack at once. They spent the first few seconds looking over each other's style, searching for an opening, trying to intimidate the opponent. These were not barnyard brutes but highly trained and skilled warriors. They circled the pit clockwise, their neck feathers raised, closing toward the center of the pit like a maelstrom. El Diablo threw out his chest and swaggered. Ivan took advantage of this momentary narcissism and bolted toward the smaller bird.

The crowd stretched to see the first blow.

Diablo leapt four feet off the ground. But Ivan had gotten just enough of a running start to meet him in midair before the smaller bird could gain an edge. They slapped together with the sound of a wet umbrella opening in the wind. They locked in a wing-flailing, leg-kicking, beak-slashing convulsion of fury, blowing away the cigarette and cigar smoke that had descended on the pit.

They landed together on the sand, rolled over and over, so it was impossible to tell where one left off and the other began. They bounced off the chicken-wire wall and finally knocked themselves apart, jumped to their feet and faced each other, pecking and stabbing and hacking, darting backward and forward trying to find the flaws in each other's defense.

Without warning Diablo was off the ground and soaring. Ivan went up with him, vaulting with his back almost parallel to the ground, his spurs positioned for a thrust at

Diablo's underside. But as he fell, the smaller cock's gaff caught Ivan in the face. Ivan buckled, and a squawk of piercing pain tore from his throat. Feathers burst over the pit, and both birds dropped like rocks. Blood spurted from Ivan's forehead.

Three, four, five times they clashed in midair, their gaffs flashing, Diablo leaping high and Ivan following. As the birds put their spurs into full play, the crowd's excitement rose to a murderous, fist-flailing frenzy.

But Ivan was just too big and clumsy to fight above the ground for long. Soon, when Diablo leapt, the bigger cock was a beat behind. Diablo was light and elastic, and when he got above Ivan, his legs were a blur.

Ivan adjusted. When Diablo vaulted, the local bird flipped back on his tail and hooked upward like a cat. In one exchange, his left gaff grazed Diablo, and his right pierced the bankiva's shoulder. But it was the smaller bird who scored the real damage, driving both spurs into Ivan's breast. Ivan twisted free, throwing Diablo. Before the bankiva could get into the air again, Ivan drove a hard blow with his beak to the smaller bird's face. This stunned Diablo, and they fought for a few seconds on the ground. When Ivan got up, the sand beneath him was shiny with blood.

Again, Diablo jumped high above his rival. Ivan saw the shafts of death heading toward him. He darted back and half-turned to meet them, but he was too slow, and Diablo drove both gaffs into his back. This time Ivan could not shake the smaller cock—the blades were stuck. Ivan rammed Diablo into the chicken wire to try to get him off, but it was useless. The bankiva kicked madly, working his spurs deep.

"Handle your birds!" Carlysle shouted, seeing that the birds were hopelessly locked.

The handlers were not allowed to touch the opponent's bird. Ivan was on the bottom, so it was up to Pescador to lift Diablo and separate them. When he did, he twisted the spurs to tear a little more into Ivan's vitals. We all saw it, and Tulia, the Grand Anse prostitute, charged the pit, shaking her fist.

"Cut it out!" Alford warned Pescador.

"Cut what out, *pendejo?*"

Bones looked at Carlysle to say something. But the damage was already done. Carlysle glanced at his watch. The rest period had begun.

Bones brought Ivan to his handling table, where Marcel and I stood. First he assessed the damage. Diablo had hit Ivan's face but had missed his eye. Blood was bubbling at the base of his bill, dripping down his beak and forming pendant globules. Diablo had ripped half the feathers from Ivan's ruff and had pierced his back. His soft gurgling meant his lungs had been hit. Blood was filling air sacs and making each breath sound like percolating coffee. He was trembling with pain.

Bones washed the congealing blood from the rooster's face, dabbing the puncture and caressing the wound with a towel. Ivan perked up. He straightened his neck, and the gleam came back in his eyes. Bones stroked his neck, and the bird purred. He stopped quivering, and his breathing became regular. Bones dabbed Ivan's skin wounds with a chalk stick to help stop the bleeding. He took a mouthful of water from his Hinckley and Schmitt bottle and doused the rooster.

Across the pit, Pescador was blowing a bubblegum bubble. El Diablo looked unhurt and eager. They were both watching Ivan.

"Pit your birds!" Carlysle called.

This time the men did not have to bill the cocks. The birds' eyes locked in a killing gaze. The handlers put them down at the far score lines and stepped back.

Ivan took two quick steps forward, but this time it was Diablo who rushed first, flying across the ring as if shot from a cannon. There was no sparring. He leapt high, flapping his wings and slashing with his legs. Ivan tried to meet him but only got a few inches off the sand and landed badly.

The smaller bird uncorked a fusillade of lightning kicks at Ivan's underside. Ivan pinned Diablo and tried to hammer home his own. But something was wrong with his right leg. The gaff hung at an odd angle and bounced off harmlessly. Diablo counterpunched, and his gaff sunk deep into Ivan's chest. The blade came out red to its hilt.

The crowd hushed. We knew Ivan the Terrible was in trouble. His thigh was broken and flapping. His left eye was swollen shut, and his ruff was plucked bald. His lungs sounded like a balloon letting out air.

"Get the cooking oil ready!" Hernandez taunted.

Diablo's thrusts and parries were still crisp. Like the rest of us, he sensed that his opponent was mortally hurt. He sprang into the air, his eye gleaming, his gaffs shimmering as they extended for a fatal blow.

But Ivan stood his ground, watching the spurs come down at him. He reached up and slashed with his good leg and caught Diablo in the ribs just under the wing. When the crowd saw that Ivan still wanted to make a fight, their fists rose once more. Speaking for myself, though, I wished Ivan would soon be out of his misery.

With Ivan's gaff hung up in Diablo's armpit and his right leg dangling uselessly, the bankiva slugged away with impunity, his spurs plunging time after time into the bigger bird's flesh.

Despite Ivan's great will and determination, he was doomed. He fought lying on his side, trying to beat Diablo with his wings, but only sapping what little strength he had left.

With one last tremendous effort, he broke free. Enraged, Diablo pounced. Ivan staggered and strained to meet him, but his good leg buckled, and he keeled over in his own blood.

Diablo's spurs sank deep into his enemy's back and scissored through the meat. Ivan was too weak to do anything but squat down and take it. The eye that was not already swollen to a slit closed dreamily.

Again, Diablo's spurs were hung up in Ivan's flesh. Ivan rolled over like a sinking ship and inadvertently pinned the smaller cock to the ground. The lockup was ugly, and the crowd groaned. I looked away.

Carlysle gazed plaintively at Bones. Any other handler would have stopped the carnage. But Mrs. Wilsmith's former landscaper refused to concede.

Carlysle shouted for the men to separate the birds. This time the parting was silent and deathlike.

Bones brought the once-proud Ivan back to the handling table. The bird was a mass of blood and matted feathers. There was no point assessing the damage. Ivan was cut to shreds. The crazy landscaper who talked to weeds nuzzled his face into what remained of the rooster's back feathers to give him warmth and comfort. He lifted him up, spread the feathers under his tail, and blew into Ivan's anus. Ivan raised his head and straightened his neck. His tongue began to palpitate.

"Get ready!" Carlysle shouted.

Bones cradled Ivan in his arms, rocking him like an infant, and whispered, "You a good bird, a brave cock."

Father Marcel pointed across the pit. We saw something. Bones saw it, too. Instead of holding Diablo at the edge of the pit as he had after the first handle, Pescador was at his table working feverishly on the bankiva. With one hand he was fanning the cock with a flattened six-pack container. With the other he had Diablo's wing stretched and was peering at the area where Ivan's heel had gotten hung up. Something was wrong. Pescador spread Diablo's ruff feathers and scanned the bird's neck, looking for a puncture. He turned to Hernandez and shrugged.

"Get ready!" Carlysle shouted again to Pescador.

Pescador asked for another minute, but Carlysle waved him to the score line.

"Pit!"

The handlers released their birds. Ivan took a single gallant step and collapsed on his chest. He would make a last stand from where he fell. Diablo ran toward him with a killing glint in his eye but, mid-ring, staggered and toppled like a drunk. No one was more startled than Diablo himself. He got up, flapped his wings to shake off the sand and restore his dignity, and charged Ivan again. But his gait was off; he got a little airborne and flew right past the larger cock. The crowd gasped. Ivan turned his head to see Diablo slide into the chicken wire. The local bird perked up. He turned and faced the bankiva.

Diablo leapt at Ivan. His spurs flashed and Ivan braced, but this time Diablo's gaffs only slid off Ivan's back. He landed awkwardly, beak first. Something was very wrong. His neck jerked, and his head turned. Excitedly, Father Marcel whispered that a nerve had been struck.

Ivan dragged himself on his belly across the score line, braced himself with a wing, and sideswiped at Diablo's head, sticking him near his eye. Diablo pecked twice and missed. He tried to get off the ground but fell over on his side. Ivan didn't even have to move; he reached over and grabbed Diablo's comb and held him while getting his good leg into play. Diablo pulled free and spun crazily into Ivan's gaff. Ivan drilled the rapier deep. Diablo jerked away and into the chicken wire. Ivan dogged him, hopping, and pinned the bankiva against the wall. He climbed atop the smaller bird, sunk his gaff into the bankiva's throat, and hacked away at his eye socket. Diablo cried piteously as his nostrils squirted blood. In a minute the Spanish bird stopped fighting and lay motionless.

Hernandez hurled his cigar butt at his rooster. "Get up, you stinking pigeon!"

But it was over. Still atop the mound of the bankiva's bloody flesh, Ivan held up his head and squealed victory. The spectators—most of them—crowed their approval. I kept quiet.

"Over!" Carlysle shouted, extending his arms.

Bones had to untangle Diablo's guts from Ivan's feet. He lifted the local rooster high in the air and pivoted so everyone could get a look. Again Ivan tried to crow, but more blood came out of his mouth than exaltation. By the time Bones got him to the handling table, Ivan, too, was dead.

I did not see the gardener after that night. I was getting my things together to leave Grenada the next afternoon, and at one o'clock Mrs. Wilsmith knocked. She brought me a shoebox in a crumpled plastic bag. "From Alford."

"What is it?"

"I haven't a notion," she said, but I didn't believe her. She left in a hurry, making sure she wasn't there when I opened it.

Four thousand U.S. dollars, in cash, mostly twenties and tens. And a note, in a man's shaky printing.

> please give to my dauter, Sharon. 1119 Morris Street Miami Florda. I am sorry. bones (alford)

I went to find Mrs. Wilsmith, but she had disappeared. My taxi was waiting to take me to the airport.

Near the end of October, Grenada's deputy prime minister massacred the prime minister and many of his followers, imposed an around-the-clock, shoot-to-kill curfew, and declared Grenada a communist military regime. The new dictatorship kicked out all journalists and locked down St. George's University medical school, with its 800 American students, who believed they were about to be slaughtered.

With the coup taking a hard left turn, and with concern for his citizens there, President Reagan quickly forged a coalition of Eastern Caribbean countries, who, spearheaded by U.S. commandos, "liberated" Grenada, its stated purpose being the saving of the American medical students. Using nearby Barbados as a staging point, the coalition launched a "freedom flotilla," code named Operation Urgent Fury, led by the massive aircraft carrier *USS Independence*—by itself carrying more firepower than most of the world's nations. On October 25, an invasion force of 7,000, including the armies of the United States, Jamaica, and the tiny islands of Dominica, Antigua, St. Lucia, St. Vincent, Barbados, and St. Kitts-Nevis, hit Grenada's beaches.

Castro's antiaircraft guns could not stop the waves of American jets surgically strafing any commie stronghold they could identify. While coalition bombs left surrounding buildings unscathed, the island's radio station was reduced to a pile of rubble, the police station in downtown St. George's was shelled to a smoldering ruin, and Russian artillery cannons and armored personnel carriers lay burning and useless. Desperately and diabolically, the new dictator ordered his army to raise a People's Revolutionary Army flag on the roof of St. George's Mental Hospital, armed its patients, and instructed them to fire at the attacking planes. The result was predictable: the Americans, believing the building to be a hostile military installation, obliterated it, along with eighteen inmates.

The following January, I returned Grenada to research an article about the aftermath of Operation Urgent Fury.

It was high tourist season in the Caribbean, and Grenada was back in the game. In St. George's Harbor, boat taxis flitted like bugs. Cruise ships were in port, their mooring ropes taut and singing, gangplanks rolling rhythmically on the pier. Creaky wooden skiffs, loaded with fresh fish and bananas, chugged toward the quay. Off to one side, sleek yachts collected like sand flies. Rubber dinghies etched the bay.

In town, stores were thriving, stalls were pyramided with fruit, burlap bags were plump with nutmegs, cloves, and sachets of coconut-oil soaps and incense. Grenadians were bargaining with tourists in creole as delectable as gargled papaya.

My taxi driver gave me a tour of the bombed-out government buildings. We stopped at the mental hospital, and he told me about the tragic trick that had cost the innocent patients their lives.

"You knew Crazy Bones?" I asked.

He seemed surprised. "Alford?" he asked in the rearview mirror. He frowned. Then he perked up. "He have one hell of a bird."

"Ivan the Terrible."

He beamed. "How you know Ivan?"

I didn't answer.

He turned to the asylum. "Bones was a damn good man."

"They put him there even though he wasn't really crazy."

"Hernandez figured it out. He tried to get his money back, but it was gone." Then something occurred to him. He turned all the way around. "You know 'bout de money?"

But I was already halfway out the door. I walked the rest of the way to Sunrise Guest House, where Mrs. Wilsmith greeted me with a planter's punch and a hibiscus blossom. "From our garden," she said. "No more weeds. Our flowers been liberated."

I've always had a nagging suspicion that my editor was in on it. It wasn't like Kumar was going to personally mule Bones's four grand to Miami. That would have meant buying himself a ticket, and Vee was way too cheap. Anyhow, why go through the trouble when you can have one of your clueless writers do it for you? The bastard was parsimonious, and he was just cunning enough.

My Secret Cigars

THE DAY WE WERE LEAVING ST. MARTIN I DECIDED TO
sneak back some Cuban cigars. After breakfast I went to a
tobacco store in Phillipsburg and picked out three stout
Havanas with colorful bands. I left the shop carrying a
flimsy plastic bag that you could almost see through if you
were a regular civilian and definitely see through if you
were a seasoned CIA operative.

I spent the next two hours packing my contraband so
they could not be detected at customs. This was probably
futile since the old clerk in the tobacco shop had no doubt
given my description to his superiors, and my vital statis-
tics were now on a mainframe computer somewhere in
the bowels of an ersatz flower shop in Arlington, Virginia.

I inserted the first cigar into a sweat sock, knotted the
sock, and put that into a black sock and stuffed it into a
running shoe so that if it showed up on X-ray it could be
mistaken for a shoehorn or perhaps a bone. Cigar number
two I wrapped in a bag from the Shipwreck Shop with
some film and put that in my camera sack, which I would
not let them X-ray. For fifteen minutes I practiced spreading open the case to reveal the row of yellow Kodak boxes
under which crouched my defector cigar. The third illicit
stogie I suggested putting in my wife's carry-on, but she

told me over her dead body and to please leave her out of my funny business, and if I got caught to make sure to tell them we were legally separated. I thought and thought and finally decided to put the cigar in my toiletry case because it seemed unlikely that a customs agent would risk pricking himself on my nose-hair scissors.

Annie looked at her watch and tapped her foot and told me we were going to miss our plane and was it worth three stupid cigars? I told her to just go and check out while I finished packing and take her suitcase with her if she didn't trust me after twenty years of community property which, let's face it, was really mine. Where does it say that it's always the man who has to check out while the woman is making sure you didn't leave anything in the room? When she left, I unpacked my cigars and tried to think of three entirely different places for them that, at customs, her surreptitious eye movements wouldn't reveal.

One cigar inside the box of Guavaberry Liqueur. Another rolled up in my Spot Marley, Rastadog t-shirt. The third nestled in the Holy Bible with center pages ripped out and for which I left a U.S. $20 bill on the nightstand.

We got a cab to the airport. The driver stopped on the way to "get change," but I suspected he was really getting puffer-fish powder with which to turn guilt-ridden tourists into zombies and take all their earthly possessions and suck out their souls and make them work as slaves for thirty years. Not unlike parenthood.

We got to the airport with my free will—such as it is—intact, but the plane was late, giving me plenty of time to sit in the lounge to consider the nature of betrayal. A little kid stared at me the way little black kids stare at white men who bite their nails to the nub. He was probably in on it, too.

At the gate an agent took my ticket, and I definitely knew she was in on it because she creased a little triangle on my boarding pass, which was a signal to the stewardess or whatever they call themselves these days. It was my ab-solute last chance to change my mind. I still could claim I had to relieve myself and go back to the terminal and flush the cigars down the toilet. Annie knows I have a weak bladder because of the many times I have squeezed past rows of patrons at the ballet until they threatened me with their little binoculars, and so now we tend to rent from Blockbuster.

"Why do you look funny?" she asked me on the plane.

"No reason."

"Do you have to go to the bathroom?"

What is it with women? They can't just assume their husbands are *thinking*. Do they believe that just because we can't figure out how to fit our carry-on under the seat and which seat belt goes into what buckle that Western civi-lization got built by accident?

"No."

"You should have gone before we got on board."

"I'm going to ask you nicely, one time. Give it up."

"I'm just trying to help."

"You want to help?"

"Yes, I do."

"Then help me find my damn buckle!"

Annie strapped me in. She wedged my bag under the seat, too. I could swear I saw her fingering my case, secretly feeling for my cigars. I kept my cool. When she glanced up at me, I looked away. I closed my eyes and pretended to doze. But when we were at cruising altitude, I watched her from the corner of my eye.

How well did I know this woman, really? Nothing but what she had told me. Force-fed facts without antecedents; a history that upon reflection was more than a bit too...tidy, shall we say; a background so full of dead air that even Dan Rather might have felt mildly uncomfortable.

She was born in a brick bungalow on the far south side of Chicago on a street with letters instead of names that looked so identical to every other bungalow that even after visiting my in-laws for twenty years I could not find their block let alone their house, and we would often inadvertently enter the home of a family named Zimmermann with two *n*'s from East Germany, so it was obvious that these bungalows were where they relocated former SS storm troopers, but Mrs. Zimmermann made a pretty good schnitzel, so Annie and I would usually stay for dinner and play a little pinochle.

Annie's father worked at U.S. Steel in Hammond, Indiana, and claimed to work in "management," which, if you ever talked to him for more than thirty seconds, you knew was a lie. Here was "labor" if there ever was one. He bought a new car every two years, strictly American, and he also refused to buy any appliance made in Japan, so the day Zenith stopped making televisions was the day his mitral valve pumped its last *lub* and never uttered another *dub*.

My mother-in-law was a devout Lutheran who looked like the husband in Grant Wood's painting *American Gothic* and liked to hide eggs at Easter and then forget where she hid them for decades and made most of her Christmas decorations herself and wound up with emphysema due to years of yarn-particle inhalation. She vacuumed her floors to the joists, and sometimes her hand would cramp-lock onto the handle of her Electrolux, and my father-in-law would call the paramedics, and they'd carry her on a stretcher with her vacuum cleaner still attached to her grip and take her to the hospital where it would be surgically removed.

As a young girl Annie did not use or deal drugs, did not have any abortions, was not in a gang, and had no criminal record. Her sister was not in any bizarre cults, unless you count East Side Brownie Troop 9. Her father did not abuse her, and to the best of her knowledge she did not live a past life as a sixteenth-century Salem witch or a Hebrew princess named Harriet Garber.

A life story just a little *too* perfect, I thought, as our plane approached the land of the free, where awaited a dragnet of cigar-sniffing, skull-gnawing DEA German shepherds and FBI agents wearing Wal-Mart suits and blood-stained belts.

Maybe it still wasn't too late. I unsnapped my seat belt, unwedged my suitcase from the seat in front of me, and started for the bathroom—which they call a "lavatory" in order to confuse passengers born after 1980. But just as I took my first step toward the back, the pilot came on the loudspeaker and told us we were "making our final descent, so sit back down immediately and do not take any suitcases to the lavatory! Ha! Ha! Ha!" The attendant, a woman with a square jaw who was the model for those Stalinist "Workers Unite!" murals and whom they could get away with hiring because it was the "employee-owned" airline, blocked the aisle with her steroidal shoulders. "Going somewhere?"

I sat back down.

"You don't look so good," Annie said.

"I'm hyperventilating."

"Try thinking of something pleasant."

Oh, well, sure. Like dancing the tango with Manuel Noriega.

We "disembarked," which used to be called "getting off the plane," and followed signs up and down escalators and through a labyrinth of corridors designed by the same architectural firm that built the hotel in the movie *The Shining*, in which Scatman Caruthers got whacked in the stomach with an ax.

Eventually we debouched into a well-lighted open area with television monitors, a white-tile floor highly polished to reflect up your shorts for evidence of hidden cigars, and many rows of inspection counters and customs agents dressed like theater ushers with sleeves ten sizes too long— the kind of dorks whose heads you threw popcorn at when you were a kid and who grew up to start Microsoft.

Annie—or whatever her real name was—refused to stand with me in line. She saw how much I was sweating and shifting my weight and working my tongue around the inside of my cheek like a tiny scuba diver stuck under ice, and ostensibly she did not want to be affiliated with a soon-to-be felon. The real reason, of course, was to blend back into the crowd and "disappear" into other false identities, to court and remarry more unsuspecting schmendricks, laying her trap again and again, until one day she would come in "out of the cold" and retire to a chateau in Switzerland with her numbered bank account and Elvis.

While I was waiting my turn, my wife nowhere in sight to offer support and comfort, the security TV sets gazing down at me unblinkingly, the fluorescent lights bright and cold and soulless, I thought, O.K., I can probably survive a long prison sentence—as long as my cellmate is tidy.

I watched the agent who was servicing my line. He had bushy eyebrows and a concave forehead. He seemed to be asking a few perfunctory questions and letting the citizens move on. I tried reading his lips. As near as I could tell, his questions were: "What do you like better, Quarter Pounder or BK Broiler?" and "Is Condi Rice hot, or what?" and "Has the subject's wife made any surreptitious eye movements to indicate the exact location of the cigars?"

I realized where I had made my mistake. By spreading the cigars around I had increased by threefold the chance he would find any one. Dumb, dumb, dumb. The penalty for three cigars is the same for one, so what could I have been thinking?

There were still three people in front of me. One was a fat guy, who provided excellent cover, proving the point that you can overdo the whole exercise thing. So if I was very careful, very adroit, I could perhaps move the cigars around in my case without being noticed. I pretended to have the sniffles. I sneezed. I reached for a tissue in one pocket after another and loudly mumbled, "Oh my, no tissues. I must have left them in my suitcase." I nonchalantly probed for a Kleenex.

When I go on vacation I travel light. Sometimes I will wear a pair of underpants for several days. Annie always warned me that one day I would regret it. Being a Dr. Phil devotee, I believed I was an expert on pretty much everything. But at the moment my fingertips were inching their way past articles of clothing that a couple of days ago seemed perfectly innocuous but now were clearly nocuous, I had to grudgingly concede that perhaps television psychology is not all it is cracked up to be.

But one thing a career in writing has done for me, aside from getting freebies from gullible restaurant and hotel managers hoping I will write something nice about them, is to make my typing fingers strong and nimble, adroit at blindly combining three discrete cigars into a single bundle of larceny.

So as I approached the customs agent, I was feeling a tad better about my chances. On the one hand, no normal person would dare thrust his fist into my suitcase of lost souls once he unzipped it and let loose all those dirty underpants ghouls. On the other hand, this customs agent had just come off his lunch break during which he had had a lobotomy, so even by U.S. government standards he was still not exactly normal. Not to sound elitist, but since the student revolution of the sixties and the dumbing down of America, it was entirely possible that this civil servant with a forehead shaped like a gravy bowl might have been hired on the basis of affirmative action and so might actually *enjoy* swishing his hands around my rotting fruits of the loom.

There was only one person ahead of me in line now, stuffing the last of a family-size Reese's peanut butter cup into his cheeks, fortifying himself. My heart raced. I looked left and right but could not see Annie. I figured she was probably in the chief inspector's office sharing a bottle of Dom P.

I reached for my suitcase, but all I found was air. It was gone. I turned around.

"Mine is heavy," Annie said, "and my arms are tired. Here, we'll trade."

"How long have you been back there?"

"Awhile."

"I didn't notice you."

"I know. You were busy looking for plots."

The customs agent was zipping up the fat guy's luggage.

"But—"

"Next, please."

Annie carried my bag to the counter.

"Anything to declare?" the agent asked.

"Only what's on the card." My wife was as cool as a snow cone.

The agent peered into her the eyes, and she peered back.

"Welcome home," he said.

"Nice to be back."

"Next."

I swung up Annie's suitcase.

"Open it, please."

I spread her lingerie over the counter.

"These yours?" the agent asked.

"Got a problem with that?"

He raised his bushy eyebrow. "My name's Ted."

"Sorry, Ted, I'm already in a relationship."

Annie was waiting for me in the terminal. It was bright and colorful and filled with gift shops. I was glad to be home, too. We went into a drug store. I bought a coconut patty, and she bought a *People* magazine. We wandered to our connecting gate and sat.

"Feel better?" she asked.

"I was doing just fine. I had it all worked out."

"Want a neck massage?"

"Not necessary, I assure you."

"Want a Starbucks?"

"I can buy my own, thank you."

I stuffed the coconut patty into my chops. "It's a stupid embargo," I grumbled. "The border's a sieve."

"Not everyone's as tricky as you."

I swallowed the patty. We were silent for a couple of minutes. Then she started rubbing my neck.

"You were pretty brave," I said.

"A good cigar is worth it."

"Things usually work out, don't they?"

"Usually."

"Do you think there's something wrong with me?"

"Yes, I do."

"I'm a writer," I said.

"It can be an ordeal."

"Tell me about it."

She took my hand. "I love you anyway."

"I always meant to tell you what a good first editor you are," I said.

"You have told me."

"I probably don't tell you enough."

"In prose, the pauses can be as important as the dialogue."

We fell silent.

"You're always there for me, aren't you?" I said after a minute.

More quiet.

"And your underwear is always so clean," I said.

"Gee."

"I'll have to try it."

"I guess we can all do a little better."

"Want a coconut patty?"

"Sure," she said. "Care to smoke?"

My Date with Princess Di

In Nevis, Americans stay at the Four Seasons, where they give you pedicures at the pool, spritz you with Perrier, and fan you with those little battery-operated propellers while you poop. Dentists stay there because they can never get enough of hearing themselves called "doctor" over the paging system.

The Brits, though, stay up the mountain, where they can look down on their ostentatious cousins as far from spritzing as possible. They stay in old great houses and stone mills converted to quaint plantation inns that circle Nevis Peak along the Upper Ring Road, an overgrown path that in sugar days stitched a half-dozen estates at the hem of the rainforest.

The English view the American penchant for constant activity with sniffing condescension—which is why I prefer to stay with them up high. I like the British. Being insecure, I find a measure of esteem eating with them and pretending the rest of the world is only good enough to serve us gin. Sniffing condescension not only feels good, it is safe. If you cut off an American in traffic, he—or she—will shoot you. A Brit will simply not invite you to dinner.

The converted old estates do not provide the comforts of the Four Seasons—rooms do not have air-conditioning or television or sometimes much hot water, but they are quiet, the views of the ocean and Charlestown are breathtaking, the mountain breezes cool the nights, the air is redolent, tree frogs chirr you to sleep, along with chattering monkeys, distant barking dogs, and occasional confused roosters. Mornings are dewy and sweet.

They are hard to get to, these tiny, charming places: up coiling, washed-out tracks, through listing villages, past straggling goats and clapboard rum shops clinging to hillocks, around herds of wild donkeys, over bone-jarring ghauts—those perilous open gutters washing mountain water to sea. But it is the price to touch a cloud. I think if there is a path to heaven, it must resemble Nevis's Upper Ring Road.

We like staying at the Hermitage, a dozen refurbished nineteenth-century Caribbean cottages nestled into a fold of ancient lava flow. Here peacocks strut around the pool, and monkeys eat sugar apples on your veranda railing. I once turned around in the shower to find a horse poking his head through the window. You don't get that at the Four Seasons.

The Hermitage attracts mostly Brits, who enjoy understated elegance and renowned cuisine. Sometimes they fly in just for dinner and fly back to London the next day. My wife and I like to have dinner at a different Ring Road plantation inn every night. At the Golden Rock, we once sat at a table with a fellow who looked as if his spine was fused to a mizzenmast. Being an American and obnoxiously intrusive, I pressed the conversation.

"Hey. My name is Gary."

"Howd'ja do. Wickham."

"What do you do for a living?"

"Oh, Admiral of the British Fleet, that sort of thing."

Cool, huh? You know who sits next to you at Four Seasons? Some guy who wants to check your bite.

One day we decided to eat dinner at Bélière Plantation, about a mile from the Hermitage and where—get this—Lord Horatio Nelson had married Fanny Nisbet, and you can still see their names in the guest register. So after breakfast I jogged over to make a reservation.

A word about jogging on Nevis. Sometimes you will pass a rum shop, where sturdy black youths are sitting around drinking Carib beer, wondering why anyone would *voluntarily* want to sweat and looking to see who's chasing you. In any city in America you would not pass these young brutes without getting beaten to death for no particular reason, but in Nevis they offer you gulps of their beer.

Anyhow, I got to Bélière out of breath but happy because no one had killed me and because we were going to eat that night on the same patio on which Horatio Nelson felt up young Ms. Nisbet. We had eaten there many times before, and the owners—a middle-aged Banbury couple—knew us well.

On this day, though, I immediately sensed something amiss. Two stern-faced chaps were standing at the entrance to the reception building like Buckingham Palace guards, and I knew they were English because they wore clothes that resembled dried bacon—Brits' clothes being designed by people who have had clothes described to them but have never actually seen clothes. Inside, the owner, Mrs. Redding, who normally smiles even though she has teeth that could catch mongooses, looked as grim-faced as the thugs in front.

"What gives?" I asked, but she only mumbled and refused to take my reservation. "We always eat here when we're on island," I said, "and we're leaving day after tomorrow. We've been eating here for fifteen years."

"So sorry," she sniffed, shaking her hair bun, making it crackle. And then she unceremoniously got up and left me standing in the middle of the room feeling completely inferior, and through the windows the guys outside dripped their gazes over me like grease, and I suddenly remembered that I was a poor kid from Chicago whose family always lived above bars. It's weird how that works, all those years of pretending I was chummy with the other Hermitage guests.

It was a long and lonely walk back in the unforgiving sun.

It wasn't until lunch at the Hermitage that I got the skinny. Princess Di was coming that night, and she was staying at Bélière, and the place was off-limits to non-approveds for the duration of her visit, so if I had been made to feel inferior, it was only because I was.

Screw the bastards, I thought, concocting my plan before I had gotten halfway through my lobster sandwich. I'm an *American*. Obnoxiousness is my birthright.

It was the worst kept secret on Nevis that the princess jogged on the dirt roads and footpaths that wound through the cane fields just below Bélière. She and I had never been on island at the same time, or I would surely have bumped into her along those dusty, rutted trails. But now we were here together, and if tomorrow she took so much as one step outside Bélière in her Reeboks, I'd make it my business to, as the Brits say, "happen upon her."

Here's how, in my dream that night, it played out: A slow, short-legged jogger, I was no match for her speedy strides, and I was trotting along, deep in the maze of cane stalks, when I heard cantering steps behind me, and I glanced over my shoulder, and—whoa!—it was the next queen consort of England. The mother country! Shakespeare! Churchill! Princess Diana, Lady Di!

"Hey," I grunted in my sleep—one athlete to another.

"Oh, hello, there," she cooed. "Lovely day." And then she fell and sprained her ankle. She couldn't walk, of course, and was terrified of the looming cane stalks and thought no one would ever find her, and, not having much reserve, she'd starve to death.

"Don't worry," I said. "I'll save you."

"Oh, but I don't want to distract you from your constitutional."

"No, problem. I'll carry you on the run."

"Carry me? But I'm so much bigger than you."

"I'm stronger than I look. I'm an *American*."

I had once read in the *Enquirer* that the princess jogged in the afternoons, so the next day at four-thirty, I suited up and headed toward Bélière. Halfway there, I turned from Cox Settlement Road onto the path that cut through government pasture and came to the cane field. I entered the forest of stalks, which would have been forbidding had I not already jogged there dozens of times. After zigging and zagging, at the far end I debouched onto a perimeter cart path, where I heard men shouting.

I turned left—neither deliberately toward nor away from the angry voices, because in the midst of the enveloping cane, it was impossible to tell exactly from where sound was coming—made a right, and came upon one of the goons who had stopped me yesterday at Bélière, facing off against a gnarled old black man and his gnarled old donkey, whom I had seen here before, slogging home, I assumed, from their day in the fields. He held his rope reins in one hand, his rusty machete in the other. He wore filthy tan pants, sandals with leather peeling away like dead skin, and a torn and grimy t-shirt. He must have been in his eighties, wrinkled but sturdy, ancient and noble, the last of the old-time West Indians, riding his donkey into oblivion. In jogs past, he had spoken to me when we crossed paths, but since I never understood a word of his creole dialect, I had only nodded without stopping.

Now, as he yelled at the goon, he was even harder to understand. I knew he was speaking English, sort of, but in heavy patois, and his tantrum didn't help. He stomped his feet and whacked his machete threateningly on a rock, raising sparks. The thug yelled back, "I don't give a bloody damn, you can't pass here today! This road is restricted!"

I wanted to tell the princess's security guy to go screw himself, and I would have, except if he wasn't backing down from a rusty, spark-raising machete, he wasn't going to be much intimidated when I threatened him with my headband. Anyhow it was really more his island than mine, considering the British owned it for 300 years. So I tried logic. "He has to use this road to get home," I said. "Give him a break. Look at him. You think he's going to hurt anyone?"

"How's it your bloody business?"

"You don't have to be a jerk about it," I said, at which time he tugged back his jacket and revealed a Beretta nine-millimeter pistol.

I turned to the old man and offered to walk him around the long way. He had calmed down and seemed relieved to be able to catch his breath and not have to chop anyone.

So we walked around the cane field, the three of us, the old man beside me, his donkey following. I thought of him as an ebony Don Quixote. He talked to me the whole way—I could tell by his tone that he was touched by my having taken his side—and at first I just muttered politely and stupidly, but by the time we got halfway up the hill to the Hermitage, astonishingly, I had begun to understand him. My brain and ears had adjusted, had fallen in sync with the rhythm of his syllables, the cadence of his lilting vowels, the roundness of his consonants.

"Hello to Mizz Donna," he said, waving goodbye. "Tell her Wadkins."

"Later, my friend." And he was. We were friends. Don Quixote and Sancho Panza. Better friends than I had ever had been with admirals of the fleet or globetrotting gad-flies or other Upper Ring Road stuffed shirts and dresses whose Queen's English my ear had mastered but who probably considered me an unavoidable American blighter. Shuffling over that depleted, dusty earth, I realized how much of a windmill the Hermitage really was to a kid who had always lived above bars.

I never stayed there after that. Instead I rented a modest house on the windward side of the island across from a rum shop.

But one day in Charlestown I bumped into the Hermitage's manager, a handsome, cheerful woman who seemed glad to see me and asked, fulsomely, why the heck I wasn't staying with them. "I have a letter for you," she said. "Can you at least come to dinner? We miss you."

I did, that night. "It's from old Wadkins," she said over appetizers, handing me an envelope.

"The farmer-and-the-donkey Wadkins? I heard he died."

She nodded.

"I'm surprised he could write."

"He didn't," she said cryptically. "But he wanted you to have this."

"He didn't leave me his donkey, I hope."

"The poor old girl died a week after Wadkins. Of a broken heart, I suppose."

I tucked the letter, or whatever it was, into my back pocket and forgot about it even after I got back to my house. But the next morning, seeing it sticking out of my pants, I remembered. It was a neatly handwritten letter in blue ball-point ink—I could tell by the tiny globs at the beginning of the light, unconfident strokes—on Bélière stationery. Over coffee, I read.

> My Dear Mr. Watkins [sic],
>
> I heard what happened the other day when you were trying to go home. I am very sorry and have scolded my security guard, and we both wish to offer our sincerest apologies. Of course, he was just doing his job as he believed was expected of him, and he is a good man who was only a bit too zealous. I hope you will understand and forgive us. I assure you, it will never happen again.
>
> I also wish to apologize to the gentleman who came to your defence. He sounds like a very brave fellow, the sort of person I would also like to have as a friend.
>
> The next time I am on island, I would be very honored if you both would join me for dinner at Bélière. I would be pleased indeed.
>
> Yours truly,
> D.S.

I read the letter ten times before I finished my orange juice. I could hardly believe it. Maybe I really wasn't a nobody. I was a gentleman who had a date with Lady Di. No goddamn wonder the Hermitage's manager was so glad to have me back for dinner.

The date never happened, of course, because before she came back to the Caribbean, the princess got smashed to death in a Mercedes. The old man was dead, his donkey was dead, and now she was dead—all within a year. Nothing left but me and the letter.

Here's what I think would have happened. The next year I would have had dinner with her, and we would have made a date to go jogging the following afternoon—no bodyguards. We'd go running in the cane fields where no one would ever see us, and we would become soul mates. She would fall and sprain her ankle, and I'd carry her back to Bélière, and she would introduce me as her savior and would kiss me in front of her goons, and we would keep writing to each other and meet every year in the cool, shadowy fields of feathery cane, rearing up like stallions in the wind.

Flow

I LIVE IN AN UPPER-MIDDLE-CLASS SUBDIVISION WITH no sidewalks, streets named after American weapons systems, landscape trucks that block our traffic flow every summer like burritos, and housewives who don't work. Lavender Lake, in Mundelein, Illinois. In a move that might surprise some fans of the United States Constitution, Mundelein was named after a Catholic cardinal, who apparently owned hundreds of acres of prime development land in a trust that was secret to everyone but him and his fishing buddies. Even today when you see two SUVs flashing their brights at each other on Midlothian Road, you know a Catholic has just bought a lakefront lot for thirty cents on the dollar. I mention this because it is not covered in *The Da Vinci Code*, but Leonardo certainly knew about it because if you look closely at his *Last Supper*, you will see that the apostles are not, as is widely believed, feasting at a Passover Seder but at a Friday night all-you-can-eat perch buffet, of which to this very day Catholics partake at Quigg's Apple Orchard and Restaurant in Mundelein. If you squint, you'll see that the so-called holy chalice is really a bottle of Heinz malt vinegar.

We don't have a gate at the entrance of our enclave because our association thought it would seem too exclusionary and draw attention from the local tax assessor, a non-Catholic, so instead we put in a fake waterfall that our high-school kids clog up every year, backing up the system and flooding our basements. Then they go off to college to expose their breasts on national TV, drink gasoline, and vote for president of the United States.

Everyone in our community is a Republican, and, in the absence of an entrance gate, we inspect all visitors' trunks for subversive literature, such as the *Emancipation Proclamation*. Also, we are for electrocuting illegal aliens at the border but having a general amnesty for the *hombres* working on our lawns. I suggested hiring a mariachi band at the waterfall, and the association board is thinking about it.

Everyone has a front porch, some wide and long, but even in the middle of summer you'll never see anyone actually *on* their porch, because the point of having one is to chat with neighbors who happen to be lollying by, and since we don't have any sidewalks, no one ever lollies. Theoretically the porches are good for Tom-peeping, but from personal experience I can tell you that the most you'll ever peep is Fox News, except from the porch of Juliet Lundgren, the Teutonic hottie who drinks a lot and enjoys foraging in men's front pockets. Juliet lives on Abrams A1-A Lane and has a fine porch, with fretwork and latticework and floorboards that don't creak, and she'll even put out a pitcher of Mike's Hard Lemonade for you to relax while surreptitiously watching her vacuum her den in stilettos and thong. Hers, presumably, not yours, although that's none of my business. The women in our neighborhood don't like Juliet much, but most of them have posteriors big enough to landscape. See sentence one. Juliet's husband, Dan, works at Motorola and travels a lot.

Sometimes I see Juliet coming out of Dominick's, her cart filled with vodka, cucumbers, and Crisco.

Which brings me to haircuts. I see Juliet coming out of Dominick's because I happen to spend most of my time at that shopping center when I should be writing. Like those in most American bourgeois suburbs, Mundelein Commons hosts a Wendy's, Blockbuster, Starbucks, the aforementioned grocery goliath, other consumption-culture global exploiters for which the rest of the world despises us but which, frankly, I dig, and, for some un-known reason, seagulls. There is also a Great Clips—which I will get to in a minute—and a Petco, which is where I spend most of my waking hours instead of working. I don't know why seagulls like hanging out in shopping center parking lots, but they probably wonder the same thing about me.

The reason I spend most of my time at Petco is our pets—currently a parakeet, whom we found, and two cats, Trixie and Babs, whom we also found. The only thing the cats agree on is the parakeet, whom they would like to use as a toothpick. Alternatively, Trixie would like to eat Babs. If you know anything about cats, you know they pee in a litter box, unless Trixie is miffed because she can't pee on Babs. The cats like to sleep with us, but since we cannot put the two together for certainty of cat guts, Annie and I now sleep in separate rooms, which is a blessing in some ways because while dreaming she snorts the names of men who, as far as I know, are not relatives, but it's a bummer in other ways, such as after I have watched Juliet Lundgren vacuuming her living room. I mention this to illustrate how devoted we are to our animals, and if you know anyone who would like one, or preferably two, cats, please e-mail me at icantstanditanymore@nutzoid.net.

Unlike dogs, who will loopily eat the same-flavored food every day until they're dead, cats expect variety and lots of it. I think this is strange because Trixie and Babs, before parking their fat butts in our house, survived outside pretty much on field mice, which as far as I know come in only one flavor. Nevertheless, if we try to pull a fast one and give them the same meal twice in a row, they will retaliate by accidentally missing the litter box by several zip codes. Unfortunately, despite my wife being a Phi Beta Kappa from Northwestern University and I a Ph.D. candidate from an online university in Tibet, we are slow learners. Simply rotating the flavor inventory in an orderly fashion doesn't cut it. No, they never want the same food twice, but—here's the really great part—you never know which flavor they do want next. Wacky cats!

The result being, we wind up throwing out dozens of freshly-opened cans of expensive Fancy Feast to raccoons, simply because T and B weren't in the mood for that flavor this time around. This happens mostly because they can't let us know in advance, cats being mute, another reason evolution isn't perfect.

"I'm going to Petco for more cat food," I tell Annie, pretty much every day.

"Why are you taking opera glasses?"

"No reason."

One night we were getting ready to feed the brutes, when we discovered we were out of Fancy Feast Grilled Truffles in Lobster Gravy, and Trixie's head was turning completely around, like Beetlejuice's. People wonder whatever happened to Geena Davis. I suspect she took in a stray cat and killed herself.

It was almost nine o'clock, and Petco was about to close. I called in a panic, and because the entire nationwide chain would go bankrupt if I stopped doing business there, the manager agreed to stay open for me and buy me a Rolex. So I raced over, and by the time I got there, all the other stores were closed, and the manager was waiting with a front loader of Fancy Feast. "This makes our fiscal quarter," he beamed, ringing me up.

Then, what do you think? In storms a Mundelein cop, outfitted like General George Patton, including the pearl-handled forty-five, demanding to know who was parked in a handicapped spot. All he needed was the bulldog.

"Me, Officer," I explained. "They were nice enough to wait for me, and I just took the closest—"

"You crippled?"

"No, Officer, but I do have two cats."

"You park in a handicapped, you better be crippled."

I handed the manager my credit card. "I'll move it in a second," I told General George. "Right away."

"Unless you're crippled, you better get moving *now*." Starting to sound more and more like Barney Fife.

Maybe while I was in the store one of our universe's eleven alternate dimensions had materialized, and our normal, non-Bizarro, absolutely, completely, totally empty Mundelein Commons parking lot had suddenly filled with Bizarro cars and green, weird-jointed humanoids hurrying to and fro, searching frantically for parking spaces, with several Bizarro cripples needing fresh litter sand because their handicapped cats missed pooping on the floor and actually hit the box.

Since I am nothing if not open-minded, I stepped outside. I gazed this way and that, over hill and dale, hither and yon. But, except for the seagulls busily scarfing down the feline turkey Tetrazzini Babs and Trixie didn't want, the Mundelein Commons parking lot was as empty as Utah without Mormons. "Officer," I said politely, "there's no one here. Everything is closed. Everyone has gone home. If I had thought for a second—"

"Wise guy!" he yelled, flipping out his cuffs. "O.K., up against the car."

"*What* car?"

Which is how, despite being well-reputed among editors of literary journals with circulations of fewer than 300, I wound up in a Mundelein jail cell at ten-thirty on a Thursday night, while half the country was enjoying *The Apprentice*. Annie wasn't happy about it because her cats were famished, so she posted bail for the Fancy Feast but let me rot until the pussers were good and full, and when I finally did get home, around two, Babs seemed mildly glad to see me, but Trixie blinked, blorted, and rolled over. Just like Mom.

My lawyer advised me not to mention the Mundelein cop's real name in writing, but my lawyer lives in Chicago, where cops have real work to do, such as trying to solve murder cases from the 1950s, so he doesn't have to worry about being arrested for buying truffles in lobster gravy before Trixie starts gnawing on the porno collection. The cop's real name is Roger R. Foley, and his real address is 4921 Ridgeton Avenue, and his wife's real name is Linda, if you're inclined to order pizza for them, say, in the middle of the night.

Which brings me, once again, to haircuts. At the Mundelein police station, there is a very sympathetic and chatty night-desk sergeant, Rochelle, who, while taking my mug shot, admitted that the other cops thought Officer Foley was a cretin. Still, she had her orders. She looked at my driver's license, compared it with the new mug shot, and said I was a very good-looking bald man. "I can understand why some guys would want to wear a toupee, but your head is shaped nice." She was not coming on to me but just trying to make me feel better, which I appreciated. She added, "I like it close-cut. Long hair just makes you look guilty."

And ever since, I've increased my visits to Great Clips from every six weeks to once a month. I don't have much to cut, but you don't want to *look* guilty in Mundelein, Illinois. Anyhow, it would give me three-and-a-half extra chances a year to bump into Juliet in the parking lot, where I could offer to help her home with her cucumbers.

Great Clips is a perfect example of how the American economic landscape has changed during the aging of my baby-boomer generation. When I was a boy, every neighborhood had a barber shop with a revolving pole outside and ceramic-and-leather chairs with truck hydraulics and hot Barbasol and leather strops and *Popular Mechanics* and Lilac Vegetal and, on the walls, black-and-white glossies of Tony Curtis, Kirk Douglas, Tony Bennett, Louis Prima, Gordon McCrea, Troy Donahue, and Tony Martin. Lots of Tonys. While waiting for your barber, you would read awhile and listen to talk of politics or sports, the clacking of scissors and slapping leather, and inhale the exotic aroma of cheap aftershave that reminded you of Dad before he ran away with the checkout gal from A&P.

If your hair was a bit curly and you wanted to attract women who looked like Janet Leigh, you would tell the barber—his name was usually Sam—that you wanted the "Tony Curtis." If the object of your dreams was Keeley Smith, you'd point to the photo of Louie Prima and say, "Him." But even if you didn't see the actor or singer on the wall, you could still come up with any famous name, and Sam's scissors would *snip-snip* into action. President Kennedy? No problem. Soupy Sales? You bet. Frankie Avalon? This week's special. Sam knew them all, and for your buck and a quarter, you'd come out looking exactly like your idol—and even if you didn't, you at least believed you did. With a flourish Sam would whisk your neck with talcum, hold up his hand mirror for a back and sides look-see, and there would be Tony Curtis himself, sitting right in Sam's Barber Shop in Skokie, Illinois.

These days I would, theoretically, need to reach for my bifocals to check out the back, but it doesn't matter anyhow, because the nameless teenager who just cut my hair knows that time is money and that the corporate manual from Great Clips only allows six minutes and forty-five seconds, not a nanosecond more, for each haircut—simply no time for tomfoolery like hand mirrors and chitchat and, like, uh, talcum? Tony *who*?

Great Clips is a spotless, scentless, photoless, hermetically-sealed "haircut-system store" whose young clerk greets you at a computer with the question, "What's your phone number?" They don't care about your name or who the hell you want to resemble, just your phone number, because, again theoretically, people could have the same name—there are probably *many* Gary Busliks—but never the same phone number, which would upset the corporate model. You have to tell her your number as soon as you step in the door because time is money, and for your crummy eleven bucks, what do you want, psychotherapeutic conversation? So she clacks your number into her box, and guess what? Up comes the stored data of your "system profile"—your high-tech haircut specifications.

But, here's the thing: her screen doesn't say "Mr. 847-555-8911 wants to look like Tony Curtis, with that little spit-curl that Janet Leigh adores, a bit of a wet look, nice and flat on the top, back tapered to give the impression of a big-time American movie star."

No. What it says is, "Number 3."

Number 3. That's it. And when you get to the chair—guaranteed no waiting, so what's the point of magazines—the teenager hooks a plastic "Number 3" attachment onto her electric clippers and shears your scalp in eight—not seven, not nine—quick rakes, leaving you with a perfectly even, three-eighths-inch (according to manual) stubble, top, back, and sides. You wouldn't need a hand mirror even if she had one, because you can bet your SUV that the back of your head has as uniformly a three-eighths-inch ground cover as the Wrigley Field outfield. O.K., now get out. Next!

Well, there's no sense bemoaning economic progress. The efficiencies of the global economy are with us, and, after all, you can't really beef about an eleven-dollar hair-cut. Eleven fifty with tip. May as well wax wistful about manual steering, room radiators, and slide projectors. Move on, sweep up, *adios*. Get yourself a frappuccino and chill, dude. Watch out for seagull poop.

Which brings me to St. Kitts. The main town in this tiny, lush Eastern Caribbean island is red-roofed Basseterre, a picturesque and bustling West Indian seaport that nestles between ancient volcanic folds at the velvety skirt of Mt. Mia Luiga. Above the town rise slopes of feathery sugar-cane bucking in the trade wind. Until recently Basseterre was a quintessential colonial town, unsullied by modernity. To walk its cobblestone streets and alleyways, to sit on

Ballyhoo's veranda and suck mangos that fell last night from Carlotta Stewart's tree and nibble eggs laid that morning by Mizz Olivia's hen, to watch vendors whack coconuts with their machetes under the Victorian clock tower and goats and chickens wander desultorily into and out of open-air storefronts that sell freshly baked sugar buns and hand-dyed batik dresses and rum-soaked, hand-rolled cigars, was to be transported back centuries.

But that's all changing. A couple of years ago St. Kitts expanded its airport, built a gigantic deep-water dock to accommodate several cruise ships a day, and constructed a vast shopping center to cater to those new hordes of tourists. Whiling away torpid afternoons, folks can now browse air-conditioned jewelry stores, liquor-cigar stores, high-fashion apparel stores, crystal stores, and even art galleries. Trendy restaurants with French names have sprouted between the airport and jetty like mushrooms after rain. Some of the old places—Stanley's Drug Store, Miss Lil's Patty House, Sheep & Goat Rum Shop—are gone, boarded-up, razed, or burned to cinders, and more disappear with each new season, most of the cruise-ship passengers never knowing they ever existed.

This is happening all over the Caribbean because, just like in Mundelein, Illinois, you can't stop the flow of progress. In my lifetime only one island ever escaped it, and that was Montserrat.

Before it got obliterated in the 1999 eruption of its Soufrière Hills volcano, Plymouth, Montserrat, had been the sweetest, most picturesque West Indian village ever—pure eighteenth-century sugarcane-era Antilles. No buildings taller than a palm tree, weigh station built from ship ballast stone. Women swaying up George Street balancing baskets on heads. Barefoot boys riding donkeys. Allamonda O'Brien's Fine Furniture, Made Fresh Daily. Luv's Cotton Store. Sparrow's Pants Shop. Mason Flaherty, Cobbler. Susan, Seamstress. Chef's Evergreen Restaurant—Bull Foot Stew and Mango Chutney, E.C. $12.98, *Welcome, Welcome, Welcome.* Chef meant every one, and he was too naïve to know you don't name a restaurant Evergreen.

Whenever you got tired of Mundelein strip centers and super lattes and ATMs and value meals and Buttmasters and extra crispies and ladies' nights and Entertainment Books and Mundelein Barney Fifes and ear-piercings-while-you-wait, you went to Montserrat. You gazed out at two A.M. moonlight rainbows, and no matter how sure you recently had been that you couldn't do anything right, you now reminded yourself that among the millions of sperm racing and clawing their way to your mother's ovum, the one with your name on it won.

On a balcony overlooking infinite sea and time, the lights of other islands and cruise ships and constellations coruscating in the distance, your limbic brain remembered what the earth was like before genetically fattened asparagus and plug-in room fresheners, and your collective unconscious recalled the hopes and fears of every ancestor who had ever gazed at these same galaxies, and you reaffirmed your obligation to all those sperm who didn't make it to love this precious universe.

But when Soufrière blew, and Plymouth got buried, quaintness and contemplation died a quick, eternal death.

Until recently Basseterre, St. Kitts, had been almost as charming as its counterpart in Montserrat, but in its headlong lurch toward progress—almost as if seeing what had happened to Plymouth had jolted the island into indulging itself with every bauble of modern life—Basseterre was changing, rushing with change, before our eyes.

So you can just imagine my pleasant surprise when, turning into a previously unexplored, shady lane on the far side of Basseterre's Independence Square, next to Wanda's Self-Serve Happy Store, I happened upon Samuel's Barber Shop.

Sam! Oh, Sam, my old friend and hair guru—so *this* is where you've been all these decades, here, right in the Eastern Caribbean. I knew you were smarter than the rest of us. Here, while your little Gary has been growing up and going to high school and college, taking a header into the rat race, thinking you were long dead, you, in fact, had quietly dropped into the way the world used to be—here, nibbling papayas and popping pigeon peas and feasting on goat stew and mountain chicken and imbibing nutrients from the breeze. Sam, I knew you were smarter than the rest of us!

I twiddled the hair on the back of my neck. It had only been a couple of weeks since my last Great Clip, but I didn't care. I shaded my eyes from the sun and peeked into Sam's. One chair, only one, but it was a good, solid, ceramic and cracked-leather old chair, with a hydraulic lever as big as a telephone pole and a coconut-sized knob. And the smell of bay rum wafting out of that shop instantly made me think of Janet Leigh. The chair was occupied, but no matter. I was in no hurry, no hurry at all. I had nothing to do. I had no place to be.

Sam had turned beef-jerky brown over the years, and he had slimmed down to a gnarled stick, and, O.K., maybe he wasn't really my old barber, but the familiar twinkle was in his eyes. He spoke creole now, but the lilt was still in his voice as he invited me to sit and relax myself. His *Popular Mechanics* were twenty years old, but, to be honest, I'm not handy with tools anyhow.

He was just finishing his customer. He flicked talc around the back of the fellow's ears and held up a hand mirror for him to admire his new smoothness. Stone-faced, the man squinted and inspected and finally nodded, and Sam peeled back his apron with a flourish and snapped the hair off the linen with two rapid slaps. The customer paid cash—no credit cards at Samuel's!—and the proprietor whisked his chair clean and beckoned me to sit. I climbed up, took a deep breath, closed my eyes, and pictured Keeley Smith. There were photographs on the walls, but they were of Haile Selassie, Marcus Garvey, Billy Dee Williams, apparently all of Samuel's family, and a yellowed newspaper portrait of Bob Marley, so they weren't going to do me any good. No matter. Sam knew every haircut ever made, and he had it all in his noggin.

"What you pleasure, suh?" he asked, flapping the apron into place and snugging it around my neck with a fresh tissue liner.

I answered him in the mirror, speaking leisurely and trustingly, letting him know with my tone of voice that there was no place in the whole world I wanted to be more than in Sam's Barber Shop, that as long as he breathed and his manual clippers clipped, life was all right, trouble was bearable, sunshine comforting, darkness safe. Time had vanished. When I gazed into his tarnished mirror, I did not see a balding, middle-aged man but a full-mopped kid from Skokie, Illinois, who, having earned a few dollars cutting grass, sat in a man-size ceramic-and-leather chair high above the glorious world, luxuriously fingering coins under his apron, believing that one day he would be as great a writer as Louis Prima was a trumpet player—believing that as long as he wanted so badly to be famous, it was impossible that he would not be.

"I'll tell you," I said, languorously, running my fingers over an ear, never doubting for an instant Sam's ability to transform my wishes into a tonsorial masterpiece. "Shorten the sides, say, quarter to three-eighths of an inch, give me a little gap around the ears? No sideburns, dead even with my eyes."

Scissors and comb poised, he listened intently, stared at my head studiously as I catalogued my desires. Moving nary a muscle, for fear of missing a syllable, he stood as noble as Nelson over Trafalgar Square.

"Make it a little longer on top, but not much—quarter-inch, tops, so it sort of stands up on its own, what little there is of it. I want to be able to fall out of bed with my hair in place, see? No brushing, no combing, no muss, no fuss. If I could shave it all off, I wouldn't mind, except then I'd have to shave it every day, and the cure would be worse than the disease." I tomahawk-chopped the back of my neck. "That doesn't mean I don't want you to taper it, though, O.K.? A nice clean blend to the top. Feathered right into the bald spot. But get the edge down to nothing, because the bottom and sides grow twice, three times faster than the rest. Should feel like mohair when you run your fingers over it. O.K.?"

He broke into a smile. "Yes, suh!" he declared, nodding his full and absolute understanding. "What you want is a Number Three!"

Lately I've been thinking a lot about Montserrat. Annie and I visited there many times before the eruption. One day, a year before Soufrière Hills blew up, we hiked to its caldera—a stinking, poisonous, hellish aureole of denuded mountainside; a steaming, boiling, gray-and-red-ground-leaching miasma of sulfuric effluence. It was hard to believe that such a vibrant and lovely town like Plymouth could exist within easy eyesight of this looming, simmering beast, only a cool rainforest in between. But there, below, at the edge of the turquoise sea, there the good old colonial seaport lay, placid and cheery and innocent, oblivious to the roiling danger above. "Let's go back to town," Annie said as we edged around the stinking fumaroles. "I don't like this place."

"Don't worry," I said. "As long as it's letting off steam, nothing can happen." I believed any place as sweet as Plymouth would never let anything happen to itself.

So that, after the disaster, flying over what used to be the village in a helicopter, spotting a church spire or the tip of the clock tower or a misshapen hunk of galvanized steel sticking up here and there out of the twenty-foot-high grave of pyroclastic debris, I wondered if the town hadn't always been a figment of our imagination. Had we dreamed it? Did such an innocent place ever really exist except in our hearts?

Then I thought of Samuel's Barber Shop on St. Kitts and the volcano sleeping above *its* clouds. Maybe it wouldn't be bad to start over, to bury the whole lot of us and begin from scratch. Bury every strip center and deep-water dock and SUV and GAP and KFC and DKNY and FCUK and every barber shop that had the bad sense to substitute numbers for names.

I decided that Plymouth had been lucky, after all. Crushed under memory's ash, petrified in memory, the most charming town in the Caribbean now would never change.

But then I reminded myself that one man's quaintness is another man's progress. What right did I have to expect Plymouth or Sam or the West Indies to stay fixed, just because every time I got a haircut at Great Clips in Mundelein Commons, I felt better knowing there was a place where women still swayed up streets balancing baskets on heads, boys rode donkeys, Allamonda O'Brien made fine furniture fresh daily, Mason Flaherty cobbled, and Susan seamed? Why the hell *wouldn't* I want time to freeze, since I'm nothing but a mediocre writer who wastes it buying cat food and sipping Starbucks and feeling life evaporate in preposterous plots and clichéd characters and uninspired similes and tortured profundities that always manage to come out trite—a faceless gray form curled fetal and forgotten under pyroclastic anonymity?

Yesterday Annie and I were looking at our slides of Plymouth before the eruption. I said it was sad, the whole thing was sad. I said it was sad, too, that soon there would be no more projectors, or film cameras, or albums, that soon everything would be digitalized and computerized, and once more there would be loss, and a generation from now no one would know there had been anything better. Feeling sorry for myself, mostly.

But, as usual, she saw something else. "You know," she said, tapping a slide tray, "you ought to write about it, about the way it was. Plymouth, I mean."

"Me?" I said doubtfully.

"Of course you. Who else?"

"I'm not even West Indian."

"I don't care. How many other writers were there be-fore *and* after? How many other writers actually *saw?*"

She was not asking rhetorically. "How many?" she re-peated. "Only *you.*" Tapping the projector cart, she said, "Put it down. Put it down, so people will know. People who weren't there, and even the ones who were. Don't let them forget."

I shook my head. "Tragedy's not my style."

"Put it down the way you do. They'll get it."

"It's not funny."

"Make it funny. Be yourself. Go with the flow. I promise, they'll understand."

The Art of Indifference in an Uncivil Age

FIRST, THE DISCLAIMER: I AM NOT AN INTELLECTUAL. I am not a deep, clear, or, for that matter, frequent thinker. I do not have even a passing curiosity for things that do not affect my immediate gratification. For example: (1) I do not know why nothing can travel faster than the speed of light, and I do not care; (2) I know there is, technically, a difference between the words *awhile* and *a while*, but instead of expending precious energy to find out what it is, I use the terms interchangeably with insouciance—a word, *insouciance*, by the way, whose correct, let alone precise, meaning doesn't arouse my interest in the least; (3) Although I don't have any idea why the smallest cup of Starbucks is called *Tall*, and a *Grande* isn't the tallest, I only thought about it once, briefly, in January 2003; (4) I never, ever wondered what a *Venti* is, even briefly.

True, I do have a Ph.D. in English from a well-respected university—which shall remain nameless, because if it were to be known that I'm an alumnus, donations would come to a screeching halt. But, face it, being a literature "doctor" isn't exactly in the same league as being, say, an optometrist "doctor." Whereas an optometrist talks regular, human English, saying useful things like "blink," an English Ph.D.

talks like Lucifer, reciting entire paragraphs backward. Also, when you leave Pearl Vision you won't trip over the curb, but leaving a doctor of literature, the best you'll do is know whether or not to put a comma after an introductory adverbial phrase. I don't know what an introductory adverbial phrase is, nor do I care, and I've never lost sleep over the difference between a phrase and a clause, if there is any, which I doubt. I am vaguely familiar with commas: they are those hemorrhoid-like thingies dangling from a sentence, for which nature probably has something in mind—hemorrhoids, not commas—but modern science doesn't know what. My university colleague Ramon, whom you've already met, believes they are a product of capitalist skullduggery, invented solely to sell lots of Preparation H.

Although looking identical to an apostrophe and just as confusing, commas are nowhere near as jolly. Airborne and graceful, apostrophes are like mallard ducks, tails down, about to land on a placid mountain lake, whereas commas resemble the proboscises of encephalitis-carrying mosquitoes, sucking the blood of unwary line spaces.

Nor do I give a hoot about the origins of a great-sounding, four-syllable word like *skullduggery*, although I try to use it and the French-ish word *insouciance* in all of my published pieces, to at least give the illusion that I earn my paycheck.

Which is my point. Non-university folks tend to think that English Ph.D.s are smarter about the language than everyone else. But you have to remember that this is a field where respected scholars say things like, "orbis of exteriority" instead of "outside"; "nonknowledge" instead of "stupidity"; "totality of logocentrism" instead of—I have no idea; "corporeal signification" instead of "finger-pointing";

and "matrix of reproductive heterosexuality" instead of "crotch." The English Department faculty lounge at my college sounds scarily like a Tennessee revival meeting involving snakes. Early in my career (if anyone out there knows if this is an introductory adverbial phrase, and, if so, it's entitled to a comma, please don't contact me) I wanted to impress my superiors, those people who would one day decide whether or not I deserve tenure (still waiting), and so tried talking like that myself, the result being that I got more twisted up in complex sentences than a drunken groom in a garter belt and required three Ph.D.s to perform a Heimlich maneuver: one to grab me from behind and two to tell us how fabulous we looked.

I once made the mistake of making a reservation at an expensive restaurant in the name of "Doctor," hoping to impress not only the maitre d' (it worked; we got a table totally across the room from the toilet) but my date, Pamela, a blond beauty who had just been named Miss Timeshare of the Year, and things were going swimmingly until a fellow a couple of tables over collapsed, and the waiter rushed over and asked me to perform CPR. As a matter of conscience and lawsuit, I was forced to explain to both him and Pamela that I wasn't *that* kind of doctor, the result being that I ate the rest of my dinner not only near the toilet but in it, reciting Rudyard Kipling.

Because of my intellectual non-curiosity I am something of a pariah at work. Ramon talks to me, but few others give me the time of day. It started when one of the professors, Gloria Gorfman, was campaigning to plaster political-slogan signs on everyone's office door— NUCLEAR-FREE ZONE. UNION = JUSTICE. LIVE TOGETHER OR DIE APART. SOLIDARITY WITH WARD CHURCHILL, and so on. Apparently it was against the rules for her to put them up herself; only the occupants of the offices themselves were allowed to do it. I had tried avoiding her for days, pretending to be dead when she knocked or, worse, in conference with a student. But one day I could no longer evade the inevitable, and Gloria stepped into the elevator just as I was stepping out. "Here," she said, shoving me a sign—OUT OF IRAQ NOW!!!—just as the doors clunked between us. "Can you put it up right away?"

"You bet," I lied. The thing was, I was headed to the lounge, where I spend quite a lot of time, not to my office, the inside of which I hardly ever step, owing to the fact that it's so filled with free desk copies of otherwise expensive text books I've requested but never intend to read that I can't open the door. Anyhow, after a nice cup of joe and a few Maurice Lenell cookies—my favorites are the vanilla ones with a real (sort of) cherry in the middle—I hit the road, taking Gloria's anti-Iraq sign with me. It was January, and it had snowed nine inches during the day, so driving home was dicey, and, sure enough, I got stuck in a side-street drift. So I had to use the sign as a traction mat, and it worked so well, I just keep it in my trunk for future emergencies. If you send me your e-mail address, I will send you a picture of it—but take my word for it, that's what it says.

So that's how my getting to be an English Department outcast began. The other professors now assume I'm not against the war and maybe am even a Republican—which would be a scurrilous charge if I cared. It's true, I do live in a right-wing-leaning suburban subdivision, which the English Department probably found out about by sending up scouts in hot-air balloons and taking pictures of me barbequing on my deck, but the truth is, my chosen profession notwithstanding, politics just aren't my thing.

One morning as we were in the lounge nibbling Maurice Lenells, Ramon, who has taken a keen interest in my rehabilitation, casually mentioned—testing my involuntary reactions, probably—that if Hillary Clinton were to get elected president, we would finally get universal health care.

"Who?" I said.

"Hillary Clinton."

"I'm trying to picture her."

"Maybe if you just put up Gloria's sign, they wouldn't keep assigning you freshman composition classes."

"I don't mind."

"No mentally healthy person doesn't mind teaching freshman composition. Can't you just put up her stupid sign? Do it for me, if not for yourself. You think I don't feel the heat for being your friend? Do you think I'd be taking my breaks with you if I didn't have to?"

"You're a pal, Ramon."

"Thank goodness I already have tenure. You'll put up her sign, then?"

"All I'll say for now is, the idea has a certain...*traction*."

"That's all I ask. Just give it some thought."

"No, sir," I pressed, "you don't want to get *stuck* into one way of thinking. It's a *slippery* slope."

"I want you to be liked."

"It's a *gripping* notion. So I won't let things *slide*."

"What's the matter with you?"

"I'm just *tired*, I guess. *Bald* and *tired*."

"Maybe you should come to our political action committee meetings once in a while. You know, show some interest in who's going to run the free world."

"Tell you what. Whoever Ozzie Osborne endorses, I'll go with. How's that? As long as I don't have to stand in line to vote. I'd rather not cut into quality Oprah time."

It's true: while more dedicated professors are grading papers and pretending to make a difference in the lives of their students, I'm glued to the set. Maybe if we teachers got paid to take even more time off—say, nine months instead of the current five—I'd be motivated to have student conferences instead of watching aforesaid filthy-rich fat woman, who (whom?) many white Chicagoans despise for being black and arrogant but whom (who?) I happen to dig.

Anyhow, this essay isn't about politics or politic correctness or even about English literature—such as it is these days. Those of you familiar with my writing already know that if you want to get to what in freshman composition we call the "topic sentence," you should just start reading on page 6, and here we are.

What this piece really is about is God. You remember that when Ramon was urging me to put up Gloria's sign, he said, "Thank *goodness* I already have tenure"? Ray, like most of my English professor colleagues, is a devout atheist and would rather be nailed to a cross or, worse, not be allowed to drink Starbucks for a week than actually say the word *God*. I'm sure he assumed I was an atheist, too, which is why, I suppose, he had never probed me about my beliefs or lack thereof, and right in front of me said things like, "Religion is the opiate of the masses." If it weren't for the fact that Ramon actually *lives* the Ten Commandments and not just blabs about it, some might find his attitude a tad, oh, judgmental.

Plus, he's wrong. For example, I have another friend, a wealthy Jamaican, who is such a devout Anglican that he

replaced the hood ornament on his Mercedes with a ster-
ling crucifix. Contrary to Ramon's theory, Calvin is one of
the most intelligent, well-read guys I know. For one thing,
he went to elementary and secondary school in Jamaica,
where the education is better than here, and then he grad-
uated first in his class at the University of West Indies, having earned a degree in classical languages. (It was Calvin
who suggested I might remember that Romanian is one of
the five Romance languages by memorizing the first five
letters of the word—more evidence that West Indian
Ph.D.s are a lot smarter than American Ph.D.s.)

Sometimes Calvin and I will stroll the streets winding
through Negril Estates on Jamaica's west end—his fashionable neighborhood of red-tile-roofed mansions nestled
into a cliff, overlooking a secluded cove and tourmaline
sea—smoking his expensive cigars, listening to mocking-
birds' guffaws, chittering of finches, coo-cooing of Zenaida
doves and, at night, the symphony of tree frogs, and we will
discuss Naipaul and Forster and cultural imperialism and
the loss of civility and the deterioration of morality and
Beethoven and Michelangelo, and by the time we've
smoked our Royal Jamaicans to their bands, we've solved
the Middle-East crisis, decided what to do about North
Korea, and how to prevent further runoff of Haitian top-
soil. We will have described the arc of his beige-ringed
cove, passed bougainvillea-weaved fences, hibiscus hedges,
stands of flaming poinsettia, lavender plumbago, and trum-
peting morning glories. We will have kicked stones,
whiffed sea grapes, stopped to sit on boulders and listened
to the lapping of waves and distant splashing of bonitos.
My sincerest wish for my fellow man is to find a friend as
splendid as Calvin.

He is such a decent guy that, among the many and varied topics we talk about on our walks, he has never yet broached the subject of religion. Although I suspect that, knowing I'm a university professor, he wonders where I stand God-wise, he has never brought up the topic because that part of his moral fiber responsible for respecting others is as unpolluted as a Caribbean breeze. Calvin not only talks the civility talk, he walks the walk.

Fate being what it is, one day Ramon offhandedly mentioned that he likes to fish—which surprised me, because you typically don't think of dweeby socialist English professors as sportsmen types, if you count fishing as a sport, which I don't. When fishermen are sporting enough to hook the other end of the line to their own damn lip, I'll reconsider.

It so happens that Calvin owns a fine, sturdy boat, a forty-two-foot Nordic trawler, docked near the center of the cove. When I mentioned that one of my university friends likes to fish, and, what's more, Ramon is half-West Indian, if you count Puerto Rico, and is a pain in the ass but has a supremely good heart, Calvin unhesitatingly and enthusiastically suggested inviting him down for a week. Even though I had a passing notion that all that upper-bracket lifestyle would detonate Ramon's proletariat skull, I dismissed the danger in favor of my own immediate gratification—see disclaimer, paragraph 1. So Ramon and I (me and Ramon?) cashed in our frequent flyer miles, and off we went—once I confirmed that Jamaica was not then in the midst of an election.

We got to Montego Bay after dark, our plane having had "minor mechanical difficulties in Denver," which is code for "we had to force-feed the pilot lots of black coffee." As we drove along the coast, and there was nothing on our right but the utter blackness of a moonless sea, Ramon had a panic attack, but I calmed him down by singing "Give Peace a Chance." Can you begin to imagine how much fun I had had on the flight down?

When we got to his villa, Calvin busied himself in the kitchen making tea and cheese sandwiches—his wife, Sylvie, being in Montreal visiting their daughter—while I unpacked, and Ramon wandered the house smelling objects d'art (don't ask). In the morning Calvin's housekeeper, Mimi, made a splendid breakfast of ugli fruit, spicy plantain-pineapple omelets, fried flying fish with ginger sauce, homemade sweet-potato bread and guava-sorrel jelly, tamarind-mango juice topped with freshly grated nutmeg, and Blue Mountain coffee. His nasal membranes having evidently overridden his social conscience, Ramon dived into the feast with counterrevolutionary gusto, snorting the last crumbs of sweet-potato bread and sucking ginger sauce off his knuckles. Me, I dived in without a shred of conscience, but at least I used a napkin to wipe my chin.

Just after noon, we reconvened at a white wicker table on Calvin's fretworked veranda for a spot of lunch before heading out to fish. While we unfurled a map of Jamaica and some brochures, Mimi brought out Myers's rum punches, plates of conch fritters, and plump corncobs sweetened with homegrown honey. The sea was a cauldron of molten gold, but the veranda was shady and cooled by ceiling fans and Calvin's lush garden. Iridescent hummingbirds zipped between clusters of oleander and lantana, bullfinches and bananaquits flitted from the railing to our honey bowls, and a nimbus of bees hovered over a koi-speckled lily pond.

My two best pals were hitting it off. Despite my previous warning and present murderous glare, Ramon started out asking questions about Jamaican politics, but Calvin answered patiently and dispassionately, and before long Ramon's inflammatory probes tapered off and gave way to questions about ganja and ocean fish and reggae and the process for making rum.

"The word *punch* is a loanword from Hindi," our host explained. "The original drink was called *panch*, which is Hindi for *five* because they made the drink from five different ingredients: arrack, sugar, lemon, water, and tea. Sailors of the British East India Company adopted the name and brought it back to England."

Ramon proved no slouch. "I thought the word came from the Spanish *puncheon*, a cask that held seventy-two gallons," he said with a false air of erudition that was really an assertion of Iberian superiority.

"Wonderful!" Calvin exclaimed, disarming him. "I never heard that before, but it makes absolutely perfect sense. I like your derivation much better than mine."

"You do?"

"You're obviously a true scholar, Ramon. We could use more like you in Jamaica."

Ramon smeared me a "told you so" smirk.

Eventually the boys got around to English literature. Ramon was so excited to hear Calvin quote Shakespeare, he almost poked out his eye with his straw. Without dropping a single line, not one word, our host recited Polonius's entire farewell speech to Laertes. After "This above all, to thine own self be true/And it must follow as the night the day/Thou cans't not then be false to any man," Ramon applauded ferociously. Possibly on a honey high or suffering toxic shock from fresh air, he jumped up and, pacing and gesturing solemnly, recited Hamlet's soliloquy.

> Who would fardels bear,
> To grunt and sweat under a weary life,
> But that the dread of something after death,
> The undiscovered country, from whose bourn
> No traveler returns, puzzles the will,
> And makes us rather bear those ills we have
> Than fly to others that we know not of?

Calvin and I applauded, and Ramon popped himself another fritter and toasted his great friends, old and new. He was not much of a drinker—I had never seen him get through an entire beer before either throwing up or passing out—so it was pretty obvious the planter's punch was making him feel chipper. Maybe as much as the rum it was the nutrient-plump trade wind, or maybe just being away from the stuffy classroom, fueling his giddy.

(Calvin, it must be said, was a veteran rummy, a Legion of Honor punchamaniac. On a previous visit, during one of his after-church socials, I had witnessed him down tumbler after tumbler of planter's doubles, shooting back cherry after cherry, and still managing not to wander off into a gully.)

"There's your proof that ol' Willy was an atheist," Ramon trumpeted, still puffed up at his soliloquy.

Calvin's eyelid twitched. That's all it was, a left-lid quiver, almost imperceptible in the shadow of a fretwork. But I instantly knew Ramon had gulped a half-planter's too many.

Cal was much too decent to challenge his guest's assertion. Ramon had undoubtedly not meant to provoke. His remark was just the flippant crack of an ivory tower high-brow who assumes that all intellectuals draw their ink from the same well. But I could see that our host's feelings were dinged. So, dismissively, I piped, "Who knows?"

Ramon lowered his tumbler. "Who knows what?" The putz couldn't let it go. I tried to give him a furtive high sign, but evidently the sun was in his eyes.

"Forget it," I said, stuffing a fritter into my chops.

"What do you mean, 'Who knows'? We're literature professors. I think we know."

"Drop it."

"What are you saying, Shakespeare believed in God or something? Don't be an idiot."

Now Cal's right eyelid got into the act.

"Will you please just drop it?"

"You know damn well the greatest genius who ever lived is *not* going to believe in God."

Calvin cleared his throat. "I think I'll tidy up a bit before we head down." He scraped back his chair. "Why don't we meet back here in half an hour?"

But I signaled him to wait. "What about *Henry IV*?" I snorted at Ramon, a little miffed now on Calvin's behalf.

"What about it?"

"'By my troth, I care not. A man can die but once. We owe God a death'? We owe *God* a death?"

"That wasn't Shakespeare. That was a *soldier*."

"And that was *Hamlet*."

"He was a *prince*, for Christ's sake."

Calvin winced, as if stabbed with a dirk.

"He was nuts," I countered. "A psycho prince counts the same as a soldier."

"You're calling the *prince of Denmark* nuts?"

"As a Snickers."

Clearly riled, Ramon raucously slurped his straw. He slammed the glass onto the table and turned to me, eyeballs ablaze. "How come all of a sudden you're ragging on the Bard?"

"I'm just trying to be objective, that's all. Isn't that the point of scholarship?"

"You, of all people, have the gall to invoke scholarship?"

"Can't we just change the subject? We're not here to talk theology. We're here to act stupid in a manly way."

"You know, now that I think about it," he grunted accusatorially, "I've never heard you say *anything* negative about religion."

"Aren't we pseudo-intellectuals supposed to be open-minded?"

"Pseudo? What're you saying…you're…you're *agnostic*?" He coughed it out like a bonito bone.

Calvin, who had been halfway out of his chair, suddenly froze. Ramon leaned over, elbows planted center table, solar-flare glare searing my pseudo-academic skull. Calvin sat back down, and now he, too, gimlet-eyed me, waiting for my answer. All right, maybe he had been too much the gentleman to ask, but now that someone had done the dirty work for him…

It was a lot of pressure to suddenly impose on a guy who has made a career out of indifference. I don't think I deserved it. I'm a good person. When my neighbor Georgia Sepulveda trips to her fat farm twice a year, who takes in Ringworm, her bipolar tomcat, at great peril to his facial flesh? When Roger Lindstrom was caught cheating on his wife at our local Appleby's—nobody said Roger was imaginative—who was the guy he called when they told him his Visa account had been canceled? When Assistant Professor Chandelier Washington from Creative Writing locked herself in the copy room and went on a hunger strike until the Las Vegas Police Department returned O.J. Simpson's sports memorabilia, who was the guy who snuck Ho Hos to her under his shirt and got his chest hairs all gucky?

My lifelong campaign to tiptoe my way to retirement attracting as little 401(k)-threatening attention as possible had, I must say, served me pretty well. Face it, teaching college isn't exactly digging ditches. It's not even making change at a tollbooth. Being a professor at a state university is as close to being your own boss without a shred of the responsibility as you can get in this life. As long as you fork over an A, you can pretty much tell your students to go screw themselves, and they won't complain. And, unlike other state employees—again, tollbooth operators come to mind—cars aren't tearing off your forearms, and drivers aren't calling your mother names that involve livestock. And, although, no, I don't make a fortune, compared to, say, aforementioned Oprah, I do get five paid months off every year with which to travel the world at the largesse of hotels and restaurants who stupidly believe I'll write a good review about them.

No one can be forever blessed, I guess. Maybe it was my time and duty to quit shirking, to risk both 401(k) and Calvin's scrumptious cigars, to finally pay back my good fortune with a little brutal honesty. Ramon and Calvin were my friends, all right. How many true ones do we have? The kind who won't shoot you if you blurt out the wrong answer about God?

"So," Ramon demanded. "*What are you?*"

"Yes," Calvin wondered aloud. "What are you?"

"I haven't the faintest idea," I answered truthfully. "I never thought about it."

They turned to each other. The enemy of my enemy is my friend.

Ramon pounded his fist into his palm, Clarence Darrow-like. "Then you *admit* you're not an atheist!"

"Really, I never thought about it."

"You never thought about *God*?" Calvin asked, chilling me with a low growl.

"Truly, guys. I don't really care if there's a God or not. I just don't care."

Ramon jumped up. "Not acceptable! It's beyond existentialism. It's not even nihilism! You can believe in God, not believe in God, or not be sure. There's no category for *not caring.*"

"You can't just not care," Calvin agreed.

I considered. "You're right. I guess I do believe in something, at that."

"That's better," Cal exhaled.

Ramon splayed his arms on the table, like Admiral Nelson over nautical charts before attacking the French. "We're all ears."

"Babbsyism."

Ramon rummaged through his scholarly quiver. "Never heard of it. Babbsy, Babbsy. He French? What century?"

"Strictly domestic. Contemporary. Not a he, a she."

He stroked his goatee. "You trying to pull a fast one?"

"Babbsyism?" Calvin repeated.

"After my cat, Babs. She doesn't care if there's a God either."

"Out of order!" Ramon bellowed.

"That is sort of sick," Calvin admitted.

"Babbsyism," I repeated, warming to the term.

Ramon, refusing to accept my testimony, probed. "What you mean is, you're not *sure*. You're waiting for further evidence. You just can't bring yourself to admit it."

"Nope," I said. "Not even mildly curious. I just don't care. If there's a God, I'm jake with it. If not, *c'est la vie*."

"I think Ramon might be right," Calvin piped, evangelically. "I think you're just conflicted. It's being lost, in a way."

I sipped my planter's, splashing my tonsils with its subtle flavors—fresh-squeezed pineapple and orange juices, sweet Grenadine syrup, tamarind-hinting Angostura bitters, cherries, nutmeg. Finally, I swallowed, the mellow liquid chilling my gullet. "I'm not lost, Calvin. I'm on your veranda."

"See, he's a sociopath."

"I mean spiritually, of course," Calvin said.

"So do I."

That seemed to make Ramon, at least, feel a little better. It was an adequately philosophical, properly enigmatic, academic reply. He sat back down and returned to his own drink.

"God is fundamental," Calvin went on, getting up a head of sermonic steam. "It's in all of us, from birth through eternity. It would be like not caring about...about air!"

"Yeah," Ramon said, raising the colors. "What the hell *do* you care about? Besides Judge Judy?"

I gazed down at the hem of rainforest and the coruscating cove. From a dusty thicket came a thrush's rising double whistle. Ramon said something else, but I tuned him out, listening for a return bird call instead. A moment later it came, the prolonged female reply, sounding like a creaking gate. Islanders speak of the haunting mountain whistler, a spirit that no one ever sees but only hears, calling across valleys and centuries. Many locals spend their entire lives having never seen the source of the plaintive song of the rufous-throated solitaire. Suddenly, from the heart of a lavender-budding lignum vitae tree, a streak of white flitted across the gully to an inner branch of a flamboyant. Another whistle—this time a welcome—and another reply, and then two streaks of white disappeared into the thicket.

"Well?" Ramon pressed.

I had to think for a second—it didn't come naturally—trying to remember his question. "Babs, I guess."

"You care about your cat but not God?" Calvin asked, earnestly concerned.

A green-backed heron silently glided by, its prehistoric shadow descending to the cove and disappearing behind a stand of scarlet-dotted cordia.

"That about sums it up."

"But God brought you Babs."

"I'm cool with that."

"That's stupid," Ramon protested. "Some horny tomcat and slutty stray brought him Babs."

"True also," I agreed, sucking cob corn.

"Don't you wonder if you're going to be with her in heaven?" asked our host.

"I honestly don't care."

"Then how can you say you love her?"

"Because when she curls up with me at night, and I put my arm around her, I hope I don't die and she gets too hungry by the time anyone in the English Department notices I'm missing."

"What the hell kind of logic is that?"

"I'm leaning toward Ramon here."

"It's not your fault, guys. You haven't failed. It's just that the abstraction part of my brain never fully developed. Babs purrs, I love her. I feed her, she loves me. If I die, she'll love the next person who feeds her. If I meet her in heaven, okey-dokey. If not, fine, too—as long as she's happy wherever she is."

"Sick!"

"Yes," Calvin admitted. "It is sort of unseemly."

"Epistemological heresy!"

"Regular heresy."

"Babbsyism."

We sat silently for a minute, Ramon glaring at me, Calvin glaring at me, Ramon glancing at Calvin, Calvin glancing at Ramon, me gazing at the cove, sucking a cherry. The breeze was picking up, tamarind tree leaves sounding like trickling water.

"Forget it," Ramon said in disgust. "He's hopeless."

"No soul is hopeless," Calvin replied.

"Well, this one is. Let's go fishing." Ramon snorted at me, "You coming or what?"

A bright-yellow, needle-beaked finch landed on the railing, looked us over, and peeped. I crunched a fritter, tossed crumbs onto the deck, and the little fellow flitted down for a snack.

"Either way."

And I wondered, briefly, if West Indian bullfinches were related to our own Midwestern goldfinches and maybe even met each other halfway between Illinois and Jamaica. It was an interesting but fleeting conjecture, and then I let it go. I inhaled the sweet, succulent breeze. I didn't really care. I just inhaled.

Why Chicken Rectums
Are More Relevant
than You Think

A WHILE BACK, WHILE RESEARCHING A STORY I WAS WRITING
on Caribbean cockfighting, I e-mailed Martinique's head
librarian, Niquette, whom I had met a year earlier in a Fort
de France restaurant, when, overhearing me order in my
best French what I believed was lobster bisque, she corrected me before the waiter brought me a bowl of crushed
glass. I have no doubt the *garçon*, or *gendarme*, or whatever
they're called, would have served me the broken shards and
gleefully watched me eat them, because that's how the
French are. For every perfectly nice woman like Niquette,
they have ten mean, lousy socialist waiters who speak
through their adenoids and make a stinky face when you
order a Coke. I do not know exactly what adenoids are,
but the French probably invented them, because it is the
official policy of their government that they invented
everything, except the guillotine. In fairness, they did in-
vent perfume, but that was for a very good reason.

Even in the West Indies the French despise Americans,
because (1) instead of cleansing our palates with sorbet, we
cleanse them with gummy worms; and (2) we absolutely

insist that *bijou* is the French word for *movie theater*. To compensate for these barbarities, the French national language academy imposes a strict limit on how many letters with accent marks Americans may use annually, after which they debit us fifty cents for each infraction, charged automatically to our Visa cards, which the French invented, right after air.

After Niquette saved my digestive system, we got to talking. When I told her I was a writer, she joined me at my table, and we shared a bottle of *bijou* and intelligent conversation long into the night. As a librarian, she had a deep curiosity about English literature. We exchanged probing questions, she asking about existentialism in the novels of Virginia Woolf, and I asking where I might find a good topless beach, and, for that matter, was there really a bad topless beach? And so on.

So, naturally, Niquette, who knew almost as much about the West Indies as Madame Curie knew about glowing in the dark, was the first person I thought of when researching a story about Caribbean cockfighting. Fortunately, the Biblioteque Publique à Fort de France had recently installed computers connected to the Internet, which the French invented in partnership with Al Gore.

She remembered me. She put me in touch with her cousin Gustave, an avid breeder and handler of Martiniquan fighting roosters. He lives in a village that does not appear on any map and that the U.S. Postal Service does not even list in its thick tome, *Manual of Places We Can't Pronounce*. I wrote to him in care of Niquette, who acted as translator, in case I inadvertently accused Gustave himself of being a cock. (*Cock* being a word that always gets me into trouble. I once apprenticed for an uncle who tested and repaired boilers and, taking his work

and my technical education very seriously, would say
things like, "Only twist your cock finger-tight," "Back your
cock off a quarter turn," "Soak your rusty cock with good
ol' WD-40," and "Keep your hand well clear of a steaming
cock." This made for difficult holidays. On Thanksgivings
I couldn't make eye contact with him without cranberries
shooting out of my nose.)

I did not really expect to hear from Gustave. I imagined
a cockfighting enthusiast would be pretty wary of a big-
city journalist type wanting to write about a pastime that's
beaucoup rough on critters. I did assure him I was a real
writer, not a journalist, and that my cockfighting scenes
would take no moral stance whatsoever—which, anyhow,
I'm weak on in the best of circumstances—and that I'd not
only be willing to show him the piece in advance, but that
I'd appreciate his comments and suggestions. Still, I was
plenty surprised when, a month later, the librarian mailed
me her cousin's reply.

I liked Gustave. He didn't have to respond, but he did.
He took a chance. I had plenty of follow-up questions, and
maybe because their neutral and doltish nature put him at
ease, or maybe because he is just a good guy at heart, he
answered all my questions thoroughly and trustingly, and,
with Niquette's dedicated assistance, we wound up writing
back and forth half a dozen times.

Although I e-mailed my questions to Niquette, her
cousin wrote out each of his replies longhand, underscor-
ing each missive with a chapter-verse reference from the
New Testament. Evidently Gustave was a dedicated
Catholic, as Frenchmen who live thousands of miles from
Paris can sometimes be.

The impression I had was that he and his brood were
good, God-fearing descendants of slaves, who, despite their

forebears having been kidnapped, tortured, and murdered by Christians, nevertheless read their Bible aloud every day and believed *they* were the sinners. When they weren't working their rocky pastures, Gustave and his neighbors enjoyed frying plantains and cockfight losers, and in the evening listened to the distant surf and the sound of vervet monkeys killing one another. I imagined that he owned a dog named Claude and a donkey also named Claude, that he shared a bit of *vin rouge* with Father Pierre every Sunday after church, and once a month or so had another child.

Here is his last letter to me, translated by Niquette:

Cher Gary

Thank you for allowing me to read part of your new book. I think God has truly blessed you with a talent of writing. I wish more people would see that we can do nothing great without HIM and that if you are not CATHOLIC you will go to HELL.

I only saw a couple of places where I disagree with or I am not sure of. (1) At the bottom of page 15- top of 16. Maybe use a different description. (2) Top of page 18. – Not sure about the guts. (3) Bottom of page 17. I have never seen a handler in- sert a finger in "chicken's rectum" but it could be possible in the location you are describing, I am no mayvun outside of Martinique.

You did a good job. If I can ever help please let me know.

Warmly,

Gustave

(John 13:34–35)

I read that *mayvun* sentence over and over. *Mayvun*? Did Gustave mean something different from what I thought he meant? Was there an entirely different word—an African or Creole expression, maybe—that meant roughly the same thing as the Yiddish word that had come into vogue among American big-city lawyers, commodity brokers, and hip magazine writers? Like our own Indian *wampum*, did it denote material or spiritual wealth and so mean chief, or shaman, or great warrior? Or was *mayvun*, perhaps, the ecclesiastical substitution for a voodoo expletive, the way Catholic saints stand in for Santeria gods?

Since my tubby French dictionary burped no Gaul *mayvun* or any reasonably alternate spelling thereof, I e-mailed Niquette to see if she had misunderstood or mis-read her cousin's handwriting. But *non*, she assured me, she had transcribed it faithfully—though she, too, admitted to being baffled. So I could only conclude that, yes, what Gustave had meant, and the word that certainly fit his con-text, was the Yiddish, slightly pejorative, slightly ironic word for "expert"—*maven*—the word I had heard almost every day growing up, as in "Some day you'll be a maven, but for now shut up and do what I say, or I'll give you something to cry about." *That* maven.

Had this now-yuppie buzzword seeped into the Martiniquan mountain streams like devil fluoride? Or was it a one-time thing, Gustave's local rum shop having in-stalled satellite TV, and its owner, after one too many nips with Father Pierre, having accidentally strayed from the Christian Broadcasting Network to chance on CNN, just as Larry King was interviewing Michael Eisner?

LARRY: We're here today with the mouse maven, Michael Eisner, who recently got voted off as

Disney's Chairman of the Board. What about it, Michael? Not enough mavenosity?

MICHAEL: Well, you know, Larry, today everyone's a so-called maven. But real mavens don't grow on trees. I mean, really mavenitious mavens.

LARRY: What kind of maven was Walt Disney?

MICHAEL: Walt was a great cartoon maven. He was also a maven on booze and cigarettes. I wrote a book about it, if you want to see the cover. It's called *The Maven's Maven*, and it's available on Amazon.com—you know, the book mavens?

So you can hardly blame Gustave, who, in his *désire* to be an agreeable pen pal, had offered up his own *mayvun*, heard but never seen, the way a good rum shop owner's wife might offer up a rooster fritter.

I got to thinking. What if life really had begun to become TV-ized in the West Indian rainforest? I'll tell you why I was thinking that. My wife and I once visited a gumdrop island in the Eastern Caribbean that no one had ever heard of, not even the people who lived there. The inhabitants had been so inbred, there was only one surname on the entire island—a thousand locals all named Johnson—and one lunatic asylum. Although they turned out to be extremely nice people, they answered you three questions behind, their foreheads were shaped like catchers' mitts, and their taxi drivers weren't sure how to find the only guesthouse on the island.

While scouring the serpentine road for the hotel, our own driver, Osmand Johnson, made small talk.

"A where you from, eh?"

"U.S.," we replied.

"U.S., eh? You know Mistah O'Reilly, him?"

Well, surely there were oodles of O'Reillys in Chicago—probably all working in the Building Department—let alone in the entire United States, but since we knew not a single one, we answered with certainty, "Nope." Then we chuckled, condescendingly if I'm not mistaken, in the wake of Osmand's provincial view of the world. How could he possibly know how big America was?

The laugh, it turned out, was on us. For eventually Osmand found the guesthouse, and we checked into our room to discover not only a perfectly good television set, but that the only station it received was FOX, home of "Fair and Balanced News."

Oh, *that* O'Reilly.

If a gazillion megawatts of *The O'Reilly Factor*, managing to find the ends of the earth, had altered Osmand Johnson's chitchat, why, then, couldn't *maven*, and who knows how many other Yiddishisms, have circled and pecked Gustave and his fellow cockfighters?

Which is why I can imagine this exchange at the next get-together of Le Grand Club des Coqs de Martinique:

"*Ça va*, Gustave? Schlep your kishkes down on a stool there. What's all this kvetching we're hearing about?"

"Lisette invited her no-good brother over for a bowl of matzo ball soup, and the next thing I know, he's eating my last bagel."

"A real goniff. Since when is your wife a mayvun on matzo balls?"

"Since she brought us out a pot when we were digging up a zombie last month. Tasted great with knishes and lox. Say, have you ever heard of inserting a finger up a chicken's rectum to make him fight better?"

"The French invented rectums!"

My grandmother was not French but always had plenty of their mustard when we came over—although that was in the days before squeeze bottles, so after we licked our knives and put them back in the jar, millions of germs started battling it out like microscopic...I can hardly say it...cocks. My grandma's name was Ida Goldfarb, and she was a good, hardworking *bubby* who made a heck of a chicken soup herself, if you didn't count the one-inch-thick layer of fat. She never stuck her finger or any other appendage into the bird's rectum, as far as I know, but I won't vouch for my grandpa.

This I know for sure. If on Thanksgiving my grandma, rest her soul, had been sitting between me and my mother, I would never have gotten klopped on my head every time Uncle Jack mentioned WD-40 and cranberries shot out of my honker. Ida brooked no klopping of her grandchildren, at the mention of the word *cock* or otherwise, and my mother was enough of a maven to know that the no-klopping rule skipped a generation, and if she dared raise a hand to me, no wishbone in the wide world would have saved her kishkes.

Black Power

HAMILTON C. LUBBS IS THE PERSON MY WIFE HAS IN mind when she accuses Americans abroad of being rude, crude, arrogant, racially insensitive, and otherwise obnoxious. I try to see both sides. I happen to like Americans, wherever they are—despite the fact that they think Churchill is a cigar, Paris a slut, *Girls Gone Wild* the height of dramatic genius, and that the rest of the world is a large shoe rack.

Hamilton Lubbs, though, pushes my affection envelope, and it is in the form of Hammy that all my attempts at otherwise logical arguments about the basic goodness of Americans must ultimately fail. Hammy Lubbs is his real name, and I'm not worried about him suing me because no matter what I say about him, he will take it as a compliment.

"Hey, Buzz Man!" he bellowed, slapping my back while the root beer bottle was in my mouth, so if I hadn't braced, he would have cracked two of my favorite teeth. "What brings you back to this shithole?"

Without waiting for an answer, he turned to Wango, the bartender. "Rum punch with Fire Mountain," he ordered, assuming that anyone not a Christian, golfer, and the color of Spackle would never remember from one day to the next how Hamilton C. Lubbs liked his mid-morning bracer.

For all the long years I had known Hammy, he had been ordering the same drink, pointing out to anyone who would listen that he imbibed only the best rum, mixed with only the freshest ingredients, and offhand mentioning that he ate, drank, slept, and doo-dooed only the best of everything. "What the hell, y'all. I can afford it, so why not? There are no luggage racks on hearses. Har! Har!"

Hammy Lubbs is a fat, crap-kicking slob. For hours he sits at Sunny's Sand Bar on Seven Mile Beach on Antigua, his top cheeks sucking up bowl after bowl of Cheetos, his bottom cheeks sucking up seat cushions like suppositories.

"Kind of early for the hard stuff, eh?" Wango, sunlight blinging off his neck and knuckles, pointed out.

"Not after what I've been through," the president of Hamilton Offshore Merchants whined in his injured falsetto, as he flicked debris out of his ear. "Not too much grenadine, there, boy. Jigger-and-a-half of rum. Two shakes of nutmeg." He flicked something at the radio. "Turn on country music, will you?"

Although Wango was as accommodating a bartender as you'll find in the Caribbean or anywhere else, he loathed country music as much as I did. "To paraphrase Oscar Wilde," he quipped, "it is not enough that Hammy addle-brained. He must addle-brain his friends." Like most West Indian mixologists, Wango McKnight was a wise man. His theory was that, in a brilliant plan designed to weaken the resistance of foreign populations for buying U.S.-manufactured dreck, the CIA has embarked on a covert scheme to send developing countries free Tug McGraw CDs, making

America seem extremely generous and at the same time
mass-hypnotizing poorer nations into believing that the
AFL-CIO actually makes better cars than, say, Bulgaria.

"Stock market down?" he asked Hammy. He held up
the bottle of Fire Mountain Estate to prove he wasn't poi-
soning the Lubbs's gene pool with cheap stuff.

Hammy winced. "If only everything was as easy as making money."

"*Were* as easy," Wango corrected.

"Huh?"

"If only everything *were* as easy as making money. For a
statement of wish contrary to fact, you must use the sub-
junctive mood. Watch your grammar, man."

"Mood? I'm in a bad mood."

"O.K., Hambone, we can see the world got you down."
Wango found a country station. The new hottie from
Atlanta, Chelsea Twigg, twanged,

> *I saw a handsome cowboy,*
> *I told him how de do.*
> *He rode me like the blazes,*
> *And his mean ol' bull did moo.*

"Yeah, the Third World." He turned to me. "It's O.K. for
you. You get your tan and go home. Me, I've got to work
with these monkeys." He turned back to Wango. "What's
wrong with this picture? Don't they know that to compete
in today's global economy, you have to conform to ac-
cepted standards of reliability? Do they want to rise above
squalor, or don't they?"

"Can I ask you an honest question, Ham?" Wango
asked, evenly.

"If not you, who, good buddy?"

"You me brudda. Now, have you ever happen to notice, I'm one of the monkeys? Do it ever occur to you I might drag out your fat batty and pound you stupid...er?"

And Wango could, too. He was ganja lean and pushups taut, and his muscles bit into his sleeves like trade wind into a jib. On more than one occasion he had assisted out an unruly patron by way of his backside, especially if said patron had insulted a gal, and doubly especially if said gal happened to be the object of Wango's momentary affection, which made it a wide field. So, if the spirit had moved him, if he weren't presently flush with restraint and bonhomie, the spirit would have now removed Hamilton C. Lubbs's tonsils through his rectum.

But the thing was, you couldn't insult Hammy. There were enough futile exertions in life as it was, and nothing would be more futile than for Wango to thump the old Hambone—so to speak. Tomorrow he'd be right back on his favorite stool at Sunny's, black eye and all, racially slurring away—believing in his heart that he and Wango teed up on the same green.

"Oh, hell, Wang, boy, I don't consider *you* one of *them* at all."

"O.K., Hammy, who's stepping on your tail today?"

"Orvis, that's who."

"Orvis a fine mechanic, Ham." Wango turned to me, and I nodded.

Hammy chuffed at my endorsement. "Yeah, well, what the hell good is having a 560 SEL if it's laid up in his goddamn yard for the rest of my youth?"

Wango probably didn't hear the end of Hammy's sentence, because across the sand sashayed Miss Honeyplum

Spencer, head nurse at Bay Town Clinic, who had come with her melodious throat to hi and hello. Nurse Spencer was a leggy morsel with cornrows and glorious white teeth and a nostril that sported an itsy-bitsy gold ring.

> *I saw a Yankee passing,*
> *I said, hey, how de do?*
> *He seemed to me just dandy,*
> *And his doodle was good too.*

"Hello, gentlemen," she chirped, sitting at the other end of the bar, as far away from Hammy as humanly possible. "You too, Mr. Lubbs."

"Nurse Honeyplum looking fine," Wango said, gliding over and flashing her a smile. "I like you eye."

She smiled back.

Two sets of chompers semaphored across the bar. Dot dash. Dot dot dash dash.

Hammy, unable to stand it when someone wasn't paying him enough attention, slid his empty glass down the counter between Wango and Nurse Spencer. "Top me off," he ordered.

"Hammy," Wango said, making him another drink, "have you ever noticed how narrow the roads are in Antigua?"

"Fire Mountain, there, boy. Only the best."

"How when you're driving your Mercedes, everyone else have to pull off the road to let you by? How you got to drive around the whole island just to turn around?"

"Your point being?"

"Maybe you'd be better off with a smaller car, is all. I'm not talking Mini-Moke—I know that would be a tight fit. But how about a nice Toyota?"

"Har! Har! Toyota!"

"O.K., just wanted to cheer you up."

"I do feel better. Say, Wang, you'd do me pretty much any favor, wouldn't you?"

"Why would you think otherwise, Ham?"

"Talk to that good-for-nothing Orvis, will you? Get him off his black butt. For weeks it's been one excuse after another. First he was waiting for a part, then the hurricane, then he had to fix the clinic generator. He's been fixing that generator for two weeks now. I'm sick of it!"

"That hospital backup is temperamental, Hambone. Orvis about the only guy on Antigua who can fix it."

"What the hell am I, chopped liver? I know that part's been sitting in his house for weeks. I know because I damn well got it here! Does anyone think I can run the largest offshore shipping company on this hellhole and not get any part like *that*?!" Hammy tried snapping his stubby fingers, but no sound come out.

"You too tense, Hammy. You got to ease up a bit."

"That's the problem with these jerkwater islands. Everyone would love me to ease up, so I wouldn't make them look bad! Two shakes of nutmeg."

Wango rolled his eyes at Miss Honeyplum, and she smiled. Dot dot dash dot dash dash dot dot.

His neck rolls quivering, Hammy turned to me. "What about you? You know Orvis, don't you?"

"Leave me out of it."

"I'm telling you, if that baboon doesn't fix my car this week, I'll see to it that he never gets another car part for the rest of his life. If you're his friend, you'll tell him."

"You notice I make this drink in a plastic cup, Ham?" Wango said. "Now what do that tell you?"

"How do you know it's not me she's interested in?" Hammy whispered.

Pause.

"O.K., O.K., I'm out of here. But only if you promise to lean on Orvis. Find out what the hell is taking so long. Remember what I said about his getting parts ever again. This time he pushed me too far." He oozed off his stool. "There's five crisp hundreds in it for you if you get me my car this week." He said it loudly enough for both me and Nurse Spencer to hear. "Hundreds as in U.S. dollars. You know, *real* money."

"Just donate it to the clinic," Wango said, also loudly enough for public consumption. Dash dot dash dash dot dash dot.

"Clinic! Har! Har!"

Hammy disappeared with a hearty hi-ho Silver, and the bartender returned to the lovely-toothed female of his dreams.

"We've got trouble, Wang," she chirred.

"Trouble?" he said, flexing his biceps. "You came to the right place, gal."

I originally met Orvis during a Nevis horse race. He had come over from Antigua with a thoroughbred named Josephine, and his riding uniform consisted of grimy brown shorts, galoshes, and a Red Sox baseball cap. He came in last and forgot that the finish line was pointed downhill toward the ocean, so they had to swim out to get him. Josephine was fine and dandy—in fact, she seemed to enjoy the bath. But Orvis's galoshes were dead weight, so he was pretty much unconscious by the time they dragged him to shore. I'm not a strong swimmer myself, but I do know CPR—apparently I was the only one who did—so I wound up blowing into Orvis's mouth, God help me. His eyes fluttered open, he hacked out saltwater, and gazed at me like I was Jesus.

He quit racing after that and swore that while near death he had had a vision of floating across the ocean to Detroit. Wango told him that was impossible. "Black people float to Africa when they dead, not Michigan."

Orvis believed he had a vision of his immortal soul being transported to the Motor City to spend eternity with cars. "God want me to tend engine and such," he declared.

He proved himself right. He had never read a repair manual his whole life, but there was no doubt he was an auto-mechanic genius. No sooner had his lungs and head cleared than he opened his repair shop next to where a ghaut drained into the sea—the stinkiest, dirtiest, most God-awfully disgusting spot on Antigua. His yard was filled with rotting fish heads and rotting fish guts and rotting fruit rinds and many unidentifiable rotting items. At all hours his property was being picked over and pooped on by seagulls and mongrels and noisy pussers in heat. Swill ran close enough past Orvis's porch to close up the throats of friends and customers alike and render them wheezing for mercy.

Well, it was a cheap location, no doubt about that. Still, Orvis's friends thought he had gone overboard in stupidness when he picked that spot to open his garage. Wango appealed to Orvis's mother to talk and, if required, thump some sense into her son.

"You know Orvis," she had said, a river of mango juice disappearing between her gargantuan boobs. "Me baby de stubbornest pickney on earth. De more you tell him don't, de more he do. But he always have his reason, even if he refuse to tell you what."

"What reasons? This nothing but foolishness."

"Don't vex, Wendell"—she always called Wango by his Christian name—"Orvis usually got sometin' up his sleeve."

Well, since we had never known Orvis to wear anything remotely resembling sleeves, the metaphor stretched not only the limits of reality but of good descriptive language. But since Orvis's mooma never missed church while raising eleven good kids, Wango cut her some slack in the creative imagery department. And, as it turned out, she was right anyhow.

See, that old ghaut was where everything on the island flowed downward that didn't have the power to climb upward. If you placed a fish eye at any point on Antigua, sooner or later it was going to roll past Orvis's porch. Since the island wasn't that high, it might take a thousand years, but sooner or later, while changing the spark plugs on a Daihatsu, Orvis would glance between his knees and see your piscine eyeball trickling to the sea.

Now suppose that Daihatsu happened to die *anywhere* on Antigua. Name a spot, it wouldn't matter. Won't start? No volunteers to push? All your friends suddenly remember they have something urgent to do, like wash dominoes? Forgot that your kid used your battery cables to tie up the goat? No problem. All you have to do is release your parking brake, turn up a Wailers tape, sit back and enjoy the ride. Because as sure as Jah created man in order to appreciate weed, so sooner or later you will glide past

Orvis's REPARES WILE YOU WATE. (In fairness, Orvis never said how *long* you had to wait—just ask Hamilton C. Lubbs.)

"You want to see Orv with me?" Wango asked after Hammy and Nurse Spencer went their separate ways.

I did. And so the next morning he and I trekked to REPARES WILE YOU WATE.

When we tapped Orvis's Air Jordan sticking out of a Mini-Moke, his foot twitched like a cow tail flicking a fly.

"Mooma coming to thump you," Wango warned.

That must have fired one of Orvis's neurons. He jumped up and whacked his head on the car hood.

"Didn't mean to vex you," Wango apologized.

Orvis rubbed his skull. "Mooma here?" he gazed around hard, trying to screw his eyeballs straight. "Buzz Man, dat you, brudda? What happenin', man?" he said when he was sure it was really me and not his mother.

We leaned against the Mini-Moke's fender. "Hammy Lubbs is in a stink," I said.

Wango added, "He think you pushing the limit on 'Repair While You Wait.'"

Orvis scratched his nose. "Oh."

We spotted Hammy's humongous black 560 SEL, covered with a layer of yellow dust, straddling the ghaut, as if about to take a giant poop. "I never realized just how big that machine is until this moment," Wango said.

"Powerful." Orvis smiled. "Black power, eh?"

"It ain't gonna be funny pretty soon, brudda. Hammy says he got the part in for you some time ago."

Orvis looked down guiltily. "Been busy with de clinic generator, Wang. She gettin' old."

"Well now, Orv, I won't mince words. Hammy put us in a bad spot. He knows I'm famous for getting thing done around here. By now half the island knows he offer me five hundred U.S. to get his Mercedes back for him this week."

"Five hundred?!"

"You see me dilemma? That ain't exactly dignity-insulting loot. Nobody in his right mind believe I would turn down that offer—certainly no one who knows me. But if I don't deliver, me reputation gonna take one on the snoot."

With his forearm Orvis wiped the sweat off his face. "Five hundred U.S.," he repeated.

"On the other hand, everyone know you don't like being told what to do. Some feller make no more than an earnest suggestion, and you think he the White Witch of Rosehall come to tie you to sandbox tree and cut off your foot."

"Pure dilemma," Orvis agreed.

"We stuck on the horns. But fortunately I got one of me big idea. How much you think you gonna charge him for the repair?"

Orvis pursed his lips. "A couple hundred E.C."

"That's it?"

"He know what part I ordered."

"True, true." Wango rubbed his chin. "Let's see. He gives me five hundred U.S. and you a couple hundred E.C. Not enough to replace the clinic generator, eh?"

"What you gettin' at?"

"See, I thought between you and me, we could use his money to donate a new generator to the clinic. Then it don't matter what he say about you, people would know you did it for the sick and infirm."

Orvis squinted. It might have been the beginning of a thought.

"But I guess it don't matter now," Wango went on. "It would cost more than six or seven hundred U.S. to replace the generator, even with a used one. Well, what ain't meant to be ain't meant to be." He got up from the fender. "Look, Orv, me reputation ain't worth any more than yours, for true. Keep the Mercedes for a couple more weeks. It'll serve Hammy right."

We all touched knuckles. On the way back, Wango admitted that when they were kids he always liked Orvis best. People were always thumping him due to his unnatural stubbornness. If someone told him what to do, he did the opposite, just for spite. The more they thumped, the less Orvis moved. Apparently his cranium got so calcified with thumping, his synapses had no elbow room. So even when he grew up, it took an idea a few times around the West Indies by snail mail to return to REPARES WILE YOU WATE and deliver the letter to his brain stem. But as sure as your fish eye would sooner or later roll between Orvis's ankles, so the idea eventually trickled up his medulla oblongata.

"*As long as he don't think you telling him what to do,*" Wango repeated—making sure I understood.

A month later a crowd sat on the sloping clinic lawn at Shirley Heights, enjoying spicy barbecue chicken and rum punches, while Nurse Spencer strolled from table to table making sure her guests were adequately spiced— pausing a little longer and bending over a bit lower in front of Wango.

After dinner, she stood behind the main table to address the attendees. "Honored friends," she said, her pearls glowing in the light from bulbs strung between palm trees, "we are here this evening to honor a gentleman whose charitable nature has made it possible for us to enjoy uninterrupted power even during long electrical outages..."

Applause.

"You all know how many times our old generator broke
down, leaving us in the dark or without ceiling fans to
cool our poor suffering patients..."

Applause.

"Well, of course, that machinery did the best it could
after so many faithful years, and Orvis surely kept it alive
longer than anyone thought it possible..."

Applause.

"But it was getting worse and worse, with no prospect
whatsoever of providing reliable backup power. Things
were looking dim in more ways than one..."

Hearty laugh.

"But now, thanks to our kind benefactor, Bay Town
Clinic has a new and powerful generator...and a reliable
one, I can say with assurance..."

Applause.

"And so, without further ado, let me call up the gentleman who made such a difference to the well-being of our
ailing and afflicted—a man without whose generosity we
would still be in the dark, but are now in the light..."

Laugh.

"The great and noble Mr. Hamilton C. Lubbs."

Gigantic clapping. Orvis, standing up with the others,
applauded, too.

Nurse Spencer gave Hammy a robust handshake.
Hammy went for a love squeeze, but she shoved a brass
plaque between her benefactor's bosom and her own. "On
behalf of myself, our patients, and all citizens of Antigua,

we thank you immensely, Mr. Lubbs, for your unselfish, generous gift of a new generator."

Applause, applause, applause. True, there were those among the guests who seemed to clap with a smattering of skepticism, but that just proved how some people are so cynical, they never would believe a man could change from a fat, bigoted boor into a fat, bigoted philanthropist. Shame on them. Because as sure as their tonsils were tittering, there was Hammy, light bulbs glinting off his plaque, moths bouncing off his kisser, about to say a few philanthropic words.

"Ahem." Wetness was spreading under Hammy's armpits. He wobbled a little, too. It never occurred to us that the president of Hamilton Offshore Merchants might be shy about public speaking. Maybe that's why the Hamster had drunk so many rum punches all night. He cleared his doughy throat again and, in a taut falsetto, out extruded his obviously well-prepared speech: "Ahem. I, uh, um, er…one time the power went out right in the middle of blending a drink, and I had to squeeze my own lime by hand. So I got to thinking, this must be hell on the terminally ill."

He shifted from one leg to the other, holding his plaque, gazing out stupefied at the banquet guests. People waited for him to go on, but as far as I could tell, he was finished. The CEO of Hamilton Offshore seemed bewildered by the whole thing. The guests started to fidget, wondering if he was going to say something else, pass out, or wee-wee in his pants.

That's when the good Lord intervened for the benefit of mankind. The lights went out. Right in the middle of Hammy's big debut, the light bulbs flickered and quit.

Now the only evidence of the Hammeister was his silhouette blocking out Ursa Major.

Out of habit, the guests groaned at this untimely inconvenience—although, secretly, they were no doubt relieved they didn't have to witness Hammy's wee-wee. But then, after only a moment of darkness, came the powerful sound of the clinic's new eight-cylinder, supercharged, fuel-injected generator revving to life, crooning energy, resurrecting the strings of light bulbs brighter than ever!

Applause, applause, applause, applause! Gigantic, hollering, whooping claps for the mighty Hambone!

Hammy, meanwhile, still standing with his plaque and looking perplexed, cocked his ear to the sound of the new generator roaring over hill and dale. Squinting, he seemed for an instant to recognize something. But then, right in the middle of his wondering, here came Nurse Honeyplum's juicy lips, giving Hammy's cheek a succulent smack. The guests roared with joy. Divine intervention at its best! Hammy again went for the nurse's bosom, but, putting too much momentum into his lurch, he twirled, tumbled, and fell flat on his bloated face.

A good time was had by all.

The last of the guests didn't leave the party until almost eleven. Wango drove Hammy's 560, all polished and spiffy, with Nurse Spencer in the passenger seat, her cornrows on Wango's shoulder, while in the back the guest of honor reclined like a sultan, his stocking feet pressing me against the door. Wango claimed you could see the whole universe reflected in the Mercedes's hood. He thought it was sensational how other cars had to drive into ditches to let us pass.

"I think my speech went pretty well, don't you guys?" Hammy asked from his leather throne.

"You're a hell of a speaker," I assured him.

"Leave them wanting more, that's my motto."

"You could feel the tension," Nurse Spencer agreed.

"I can't get over how much money that son of a bitch socked away," Hammy said.

"Who?" Wango wanted to know.

"Orvis, who do you think? Can you imagine how much dough that monkey must have to donate a new generator to the clinic in my name? Jesus H., he must have ripped us all off for years!"

Wango squinted into the rearview mirror. "Hammy, why you calling Orvis a monkey now? Didn't he just do something nice for you to show how sorry he is to take so long with the car? With no gain to himself and complete anonymity, so there can never be a question of you sharing any glory?"

"No gain to himself! Har! Har! Don't be naïve, boy."

"Out of order!"

Hammy knocked on his plaque. "For the price of a cheap piece of plywood and brass, he thinks I'll never again hold up any of his damn parts. Does he think I'm stupid? Does he really think he can outsmart *me*?"

No reply.

"We'll see who's going to outsmart who," Hammy huffed.

Everyone was silent, until the Mercedes began its climb up Admiral Hill.

"Goose it, boy," Hammy commanded.

"What for?"

"Doesn't it seem kind of sluggish?"

"Feels fine to me, Ham."

"She strains with the air conditioning on, too," Hammy observed, as the Mercedes whined upward.

"Sounds all right to me," Nurse Spencer said, squeezing Wango's knee bone.

"It's not working too hard?" Hammy pressed. "Seems like it hasn't been the same since I got it back."

"She's perfect, Ham," Wango assured him. "Did you check under the hood?"

"What the hell for? I'm a thinker, not a grease monkey. But I swear to God, since I got it back it rides like a frigging Mini-Moke."

Wango grabbed a CD from the console and shoved it into the dashboard.

Danke schön,
My darlin', danke schön...

"Oh, goodie, Wayne Newton!" he exclaimed. "Next to Bob Marley, me favorite." He turned up the volume so Hammy wouldn't have to bother himself with strange engine sounds.

Bei mir bist du schön,
Please let me explain,
Bei mir bist du schön means that
you're graaand...

I knew what Wango was thinking, and he probably knew I was thinking the same: *Would be a shame to ruin Hammy's special night, eh?*

Sometimes It's the Other Way Around

DESPITE WHAT HAPPENED, I WON'T TELL YOU THE ISLAND'S real name, only that in an obvious effort to encourage tourism, it conveniently forgets to mention the $30 per person departure tax—cash only—until you're ready to board the plane. But the government is so progressive-thinking, they insist that the cashier always say, "Hurry back."

If absolutely necessary, they'll accept E.C. dollars, which government ministers encourage ordinary citizens to favor over U.S. dollars, but which they themselves don't like because if any bills happen to accidentally go through the wash, they come out looking like a Jackson Pollack painting during one of his alcoholic benders.

Officially, the exchange rate is $2.60 E.C. per $1.00 U.S., but in practice this fluctuates according to how many cruise ships happen to be in port that day and how fat your wife's thighs are. If you walk around town wearing flip-flops while slurping a frozen margarita, you will wind up paying five hundred bucks for a crab salad sandwich.

I have a handy, infallible system for quickly calculating the exchange rate on any given day, and you are free to use it. You divide the posted price by the distance from the equator to the planet Neptune when the earth is in full apogee, multiplied by how many times room service goes back and forth to bring you a glass of ice, one cube at a time. Subtract the number of power outages that day from the number of times the customs inspector rotates his rubber stamp on your form, and add the number of minutes the directory-assistance operator takes to find your number while chatting it up with her colleague about last night's jump-up at Cal's Friday Night Rip.

I will call this island "St. George," because it used to be a British colony, as did most of the world, and if you ever tried to eat beef in England or owned a Jaguar you understand why they couldn't hang on to it. My art-collecting friend, "Greg"—a widower with a four-year-old son, Stephen—owned one of the oldest and most respected plantation-house inns on St. George, "Greystone," a 300-year-old stone beauty nestled on the brow of a mountain overlooking sloping cane fields and turquoise sea. When on island, British royalty would never stay anywhere but at Greystone because: (1) its original owner, Greg's ancestor, was himself a bit of British blueblood; (2) Greg delivered good, old-fashioned upper-crust service, including tea and crumpets on a shaded terrace; (3) situated at the edge of St. George's rainforest at the end of a tortuous path, Greystone required a bit of effort and inconvenience to get to and, therefore, (4) Americans, whom the British secretly loathe, tended not to stay there.

Greg himself, while almost as stuffy as his aristocratic counterparts, was a thoroughly decent chap, as much a part of the St. George soil as Greystone itself. If there was ever a local cause needing money or advice or assistance, Greg was there, unhesitatingly. Maybe somewhere in the recesses of his stuffed-shirt heart he still considered himself British, but in words and deeds he was pure St. Georgian. It was Greg's family who had trumpeted the way for the island's independence in the seventies, and now it was Greg himself who sat long into nights writing letters to cousins in England asking for grants with which to build new roads, schools, and clinics on his beloved island.

When one of the old cousins croaked, Greg unexpectedly inherited 100,000 pounds, a small fortune back then, certainly on St. George, where there was a 44 percent unemployment rate and the other 56 percent worked for the so-called government. The island's main town, Elizabeth, was a quaint eighteenth-century port community, but it had deteriorated badly. It consisted of one narrow road, on which cars had to drive onto the curb to let others pass, about twenty stone buildings with sagging balconies and fractured fretwork, and a dilapidated pier. Having endured hurricanes, earthquakes, floods, the collapse of cotton, sugar, and slave markets, and prolonged colonial and tourist neglect, Elizabeth was now a swaybacked nag. On hearing about his sudden windfall, Greg's first thought was to put his new money into bucking up the old girl with a bit of makeover and massage.

So he bought a vacant, two-story, former coffee-weighing building on Sea Street, bought it without haggling—the owners, living in Montreal, were as thrilled with the offer as Greg himself had been with his inheritance—and proceeded to plan the property's facelift, which he hoped would spark further investment in town. His idea was simple, rational, and progressive. Contrary to what his island administration friends had hoped, instead of merely dropping his money into the national coffers for vague social "benefits"—he well knew the fate of his donation in that lightless abyss—he decided to invest the money to create new private-sector jobs and, at the same time, uplift the look, feel, and self-respect of Elizabethans. Greg may have been philanthropic to a fault, but he was smart enough to know that free-market capitalism far outweighed the inefficiencies of a bloated central government, especially one bloated by former colonial boot wipes.

What he did was, he completely rehabbed that old coffee building and turned it into a stunning fine-arts gallery, a showplace, fit to compete with any on St. Martin or San Juan or even Miami. His dream was that St. George's would blossom into a world-renowned art center and, at the same time, local children would learn about painting and sculpture, maybe piquing their interest for artistic careers. He envisioned bringing vanloads of his Greystone guests to his refurbished building. More investors would come, open more galleries, attract more high-disposable-income visitors with refined tastes, which, in turn, would stimulate even more growth and provide even more respectable jobs—jobs that did not mire locals in low-paying, bureaucratic paper-shuffling, or demeaning tourism-service work.

As investments go, it was risky—some good businessmen might say stupid—but Greg wasn't a bean counter, he was a St. Georgian, and he had happened to wake up one day to find himself 100,000 pounds richer for doing nothing, so the word *risk*, in this case, meant nothing, and anyhow he felt a sense of destiny about it, maybe a long-overdue gesture of reparation for those wretched days of slavery.

It took almost two years to rehab the coffee building, but that's the West Indies. In the meantime, he put to work local masons and carpenters and plasterers and plumbers and painters; tile layers and electricians and landscapers and glazers—not specialists but semi-skilled laborers who usually worked off island but returned to work for Greg because he insisted on St. George labor and paid them well.

From Wabash Pinfold Hardw'r Store he bought sinks and toilets and air conditioners and cabinets and latches and lights. He imagined that with the success of his gallery, St. George would need to open more supply stores—more non-hotel jobs—and he even dreamed of funding a local technical school for architecture and construction, so the rest of the Caribbean would demand St. Georgians, the finest tradesmen and women in the West Indies.

He named his showplace Masterpiece Galleries of St. George because he wanted the island's name to be associated with refinement. It was high time locals had something to feel good about. He hired three local women, Carmen, Needa, and Lill, fitted them with smart, professional-looking, tailor-made dresses, pastel yellow and breezy, with custom nametags sewn, not pinned, on their lapels—which not only looked good but proved his confidence in their sales longevity. He trained them how to show and sell paintings and sculpture—the selling itself a fine art—and believed that those skills would benefit them in all aspects of their lives. He taught them the correct terminology, showed them the right way to stand, how to make effective gestures, explained when to talk, when to listen, and when to take out their order forms. He made sure their linen was pressed and buttons buttoned. He demonstrated the way to ask leading questions, how to detect serious interest and keep the prospects focused, explained the importance of ushering would-be buyers into the private viewing room, taught them how to close the sale ("Congratulations on your exquisite taste. Will that be cash or credit card?"). How never to stand in front of a piece of artwork, never to hold a pen until writing up the order, to always have fingernails manicured and polished. How to discreetly suggest a piece's investment potential without making any claims.

When his saleswomen were prim, proper, and primed, he held his grand opening, an exhibition of a brilliant and renowned modern impressionist, Karl Merklein, whose acrylic-on-canvases captured West Indian life in fresh, whimsical detail. He had sent out invitations weeks earlier to every guest who had ever stayed at Greystone. Now St. George's harbor was clustered with fluttering yachts and dinghies scoring the bay. It was a starry tropical night, hook-mooned, with the aroma of bay rum and coconut shrimps and the heady rhythms of Tall Man steel band careening down Main Street and up Mt. George, pleasantly mingling, in Masterpiece Gallery, with the smell of fresh stucco, paint, and Angostura bitters.

The guests wore white and pastels. At the door, Carmen pinned hibiscus blossoms on the gentlemen's lapels and offered them to the ladies for their hair. Merklein was there, of course, and he answered questions and laughed breezily and was pleasant and handsome in his pony tail, tanned and confident, and he sold eleven paintings that night and took commissions on five more. One North Carolina woman invited him to her yacht to give him "inspiration."

So the grand opening was a huge success, a smash, and near dawn Greg fell into exhausted sleep knowing he had fulfilled his life's purpose. No doubt Carmen, Needa, and Lill felt so, too.

Everything went terrifically well for the next three months—better than even Greg had expected—so well that he hired another saleswoman and began to title-search the adjoining property. It was while he was in the Buildings Department records room, poring over musty land documents, that Hanley Benson's secretary tapped him on his shoulder.

"The Minister of Commerce would like to see you," she said, sucking a lime.

"When?"

"I think the sooner the better."

The government building was a former seaside hotel, which resembled a day motel for cheaters, with crumbling-concrete balconies, plywood windows, loose Celotex over-hang panels, and curlicue wrought-iron railings, painted, more or less alternately, red and powder blue. On what used to be the hotel sign someone had painted a crude, now faded, St. George's flag. On one side, the building overlooked a stinking ghaut and, on the other, a course, tumbledown cemetery where goats and chickens wandered among blossomless weeds, bramble, and sooty grave-stones, inscriptions worn smooth by centuries of buffeting winds and hurricane tides.

Despite window air conditioners, the government rooms were close and stifling. Hanley Benson had a corner office overlooking Jelly W. Notions Centre. The commerce minister rocked in his chair, scratched his close beard, and folded his pudgy fingers over stretched buttonholes. His air conditioner was on full blast, rippling his weighted-down desk papers.

"How goes the store?" he asked, after taking a moment to write something.

"Gallery," Greg corrected, raising his voice over the air conditioner.

"How it goes?" His cheeks were fat and oily, his eyes small and catfish murky.

"Wonderfully well. But you know that."

"Yes, I heard. Lill."

"What's up, Hanley?"

"She sold three big paintings, eh? Merkleins."

"She's good. Has a brilliant future, I dare say."

"Said you show her how to fold her hands, just so, eh? How to stand so she don't look like she just got off the boat from Africa. Keep her back straight, fingers like so, no rocking back and forth, no stains on dress, hair in place, always smiling, eh? Yes, gentleman, sir, no, misses, ma'am."

Greg knew he had to tread lightly. "She's going to make money. She enjoys it."

"You a perfectionist, Greg." Rocking back and forth, he peeked at Greg with a finch-like glance. "Must be hell on your nerves."

"It's kept Greystone in business."

"You did a good job at the new store. Looks plenty smart."

"I just hired Alma Lawrence."

"Alma! How come always gal, never men, eh?"

"Women are naturals at selling art. Especially pretty women. None prettier than on St. George."

He twirled his pinky in his ear. "You right about that."

Greg glanced at his watch.

"Always in a hurry, eh? A perfectionist." He clucked. "Showing ladies how to do it. Yes, sir, no, madam. Whatever you say, mister and missus."

"Something on your mind, Hanley?"

"O.K., man, I'll get to the point. We had a board meeting last night, you know."

"First Monday of the month."

"We made a decision about art."

Greg suddenly felt sick.

"We...*they* decided we should promote local art. Not just you, I mean. Everybody. Island-wide. St. George art. You for that, aren't you?"

"Local art?" Greg asked incredulously.

"Yes, man, local art. Local art. St. George artists."

"*What* St. George artists?"

The commerce minister frowned. He sucked his teeth. "That's the point, man. How we know if we don't look?"

"I've lived here all my life. The only artist I ever knew was Peg, the old woman who carved coconut heads, and she's dead."

"What's wrong with coconut heads? That's authentic, man. Peg's coconuts could be worth something sometime, if they promoted right."

Greg stared at the minister's wide nose, his fat head. "This is a joke, right? The board decided to play a joke on me?"

"No joke, man. Peg dead, but how about Jasmine Carmichael's little dolls?"

"Straw dolls?"

"Native art, man. Look at the Navajos."

"Navajos?"

"Rugs, man. This you business. Bone up."

Greg chuckled uneasily. "The board wants me to sell dolls?" Not believing that's what Hanley meant, of course.

"Not if you don't want to. Is entirely up to you. Free enterprise, you know. We ain't communists, eh?"

"So this is just a suggestion."

"To encourage you to sell local art. Nothing mandatory, don't worry."

Greg leaned over. "You're not kidding, are you? You really want me to sell coconut heads and straw dolls?"

"Look, you never know what artistic geniuses we have right here among us, who only need a little encouragement. You all for that, eh?"

"Nothing wrong with craft art—in a crafts store."

The minister pouted. "But not for you, eh? You like *fine* art. *European* art. *American* art. *Canada* art."

Greg got up, extended his hand. "Jolly good, Hanley. I'll consider it. Maybe we can figure something out. Tell them I'm open-minded about it. We'll think of something."

The commerce minister shook Greg's hand. "I ain't done. Better sit again."

Greg leaned against the chair, but Hanley wouldn't talk until Greg sat, so he sat.

The minister puckered. "We...*they* signed a motion to impose a surtax on any non–St. George art."

"Surtax?"

"An...inducement, let's say."

Greg's throat was closing. "How much?"

Hanley clicked his retractable pen a few times. He forced himself to look into his guest's eyes. "Forty percent."

Greg got up, turned off the air conditioner. He knew Hanley would see this as insolence. Without sitting back down, he said, "I don't think I heard you correctly. Too much damn noise in here."

Insulted, Hanley found his courage. "Forty percent on any non–St. George art."

Greg bent down and got his face in front of the minister's. "This *is* a practical joke, isn't it?"

"The feeling is, you sell a nice European painting for a couple thousand minimum, what's a few hundred more?"

"Lord Jesus."

"No surtax on local art," Hanley said with a wave, making sure Greg understood the silver lining.

Greg felt himself flush. His spine stiffened. He grabbed Hanley's message spike, turned it upside down, and thrust it deep into his desk pad. The commerce minister recoiled. "Where's Cal?" Greg snarled.

"Don't get vex at me, man. I was against it, but they voted me down."

"Where's Cal?!"

"I don't know. Doing prime minister stuff, I guess."

Greg stormed out. His temper had not simmered when, half an hour later, murder still in his heart, he found the prime minister at his grocery store, taking inventory, his shirt pocket overflowing with folded and crumpled papers, three pens, and a lottery ticket. He was counting jars of Nescafé when Greg stepped between him and the shelf.

"You heard?" Calvin said.

"You're mad."

"Don't get vex at me, man. I voted against it, but they voted me down."

He drilled the prime minister a death gaze. But unlike the commerce minister, Calvin did not look away. Greg already knew it was not a question of a bribe, or someone would have brought it up in advance. He knew every one of these politicians and their families. His son played with their kids. His wife had been a St. Georgian; his boy, Stephen, was half one by blood, full one every other way. Greg broke bread and went to church with them. He fed them free meals every month at Greystone. He hosted

taxi-driver breakfasts. He waxed philosophical and geo-
political and spiritual with them and their wives on his
terrace.

He knew they would all deny voting for it, every one of
them, but in the prime minister's gaze Greg recognized a
rock-hard, former-slave-now-free-man-we-tell-you-what-
to-do-not-the-other-way-around intransigence. Their minds
were made up.

"It's insane," he said. It was all he could think of. He already knew he was beaten. "Insane." Just to go on record.

"Actually the premise is sound—even though I voted
against it, you know. We're friends, I can level with you.
How you think the citizens feel, you selling art from foreign people painting all kind of Caribbean scenes? It seem
wrong to some people. All we saying is a little civic inclu-
sion, that's all, a little encouragement."

"It's not that kind of gallery."

"Maybe one section."

Greg had no more words. He just gazed stupefied at the
prime minister, pencil stub in his stupid ear, Nescafé in his
stupid hand, stupid thumb smeared with graphite where it
had rubbed off stupid old prices to apply stupid new ones.

"Forty percent won't mean much to your clientele. You
don't have to show it on your invoice, so they will never
know. I give you my personal promise, they will never
know." His eyes twinkled. "They will only think the paintings more valuable, eh?" He reached around Greg to
reshelf his Nescafés. "Maybe you actually sell more that
way, eh? Maybe it's a good marketing ploy."

Greg slunk away.

The next morning he put up a hand-painted OUT OF
BUSINESS sign on Masterpiece's door, paid the shell-shocked

saleswomen what he owed them plus $200 bonuses, and started taking his paintings off the wall. Lill melted away crying into a handkerchief, Needa hugged him and said it was a damn shame, and Carmen made two fists and vowed she would leave this blasted island and never come back.

But it was Greg who left first. He put his building up for sale but, knowing it would probably rot before anyone would ever take an interest in it again, didn't wait for results. Within a month he closed Greystone, laying off his gardener, laundress, two cooks, three waitresses, handyman, and his longtime secretary, Charlotte. He closed his account at St. George bank, took his cash, and moved to southern France without a forwarding phone number.

A few months later, he wrote me a long, sad letter, explaining everything, saying he was sorry he had "acted intemperately," that his pride was his downfall, sorry he had caused his employees and friends pain, but that he had done it for Stephen. When he was standing in Cal's grocery store and listening to the babble, all he could think about was saving his son.

He said Stephen was lonely and missed his friends. Greg was lonely too, but he knew that would get better. It broke his heart to see Stephen unhappy, but he wouldn't go back. Maybe he had made a mistake, but he'd do the best he could. Maybe they'd get used to France.

I wrote back saying, "Well, when it comes to finding small-minded countries, you certainly know how to pick them." I told him he should try Israel; at least Stephen would learn how to fight.

The rainforest quickly reclaimed Greg's old plantation inn. Within months it looked like the 300-year-old relic that, in truth, it always had been. A decade later a young

Swiss couple bought it and tried to convert it to a bed and breakfast, without success. Like Greg, they abandoned their dream, and today the crumbling stone walls peek out of thick underbrush like a Mayan ruin.

A couple of years after Greg's departure, as promised, Carmen also left St. George for good, to live with her cousin in Atlanta. She married a lawyer-turned-investment banker, lived in a 9,000-square-foot mansion, and had three brilliant, over-achieving children, the eldest of whom became the best-selling country music sensation Chelsea Twigg—the very same Atlanta hottie whose voice, twenty-one years after Greg's self-imposed exile, twanged over Wango McKnight's boom box, and whom Hammy Lubbs demanded be made louder at Sunny's Beach Bar on Antigua.

The same country music superstar who had a wildly successful concert tour through Europe and who, after a concert in Nice, France, met a good-looking young British journalist named Stephen, who, like she, loved great art and who invited her to fly to Paris to visit the Louvre, and who fell in love with Chelsea even before discovering that they both had roots in the Eastern Caribbean. The same Stephen and Chelsea who got married and named their first baby Karma.

People want to know if this really happened. Trust me, I'm not good enough to make this stuff up.

Where Satan Works

WHEN I WAS A TEENAGER, I SAW A LOW-BUDGET HORROR movie called *Island of the Doomed*, starring a blacklisted communist actor who apparently had not eaten for several years and had eczema. In the film, a young couple, an American private pilot and his Asian girlfriend, crash land on an uncharted, fog-engulfed Caribbean island inhabited by, of all people, Satan. They never say exactly what the Prince of Darkness was doing there. Maybe he was scouting out a time-share development. They also never say why the young couple was out flying under cover of night, but based on their shoveling munchies into each other's faces while they should have been watching the altimeter, I have my suspicions.

In any event, the Antichrist comes on to the sexy Chinese girlfriend, and the American pilot gets ticked off and barricades him in a cave with crosses made of driftwood—he doesn't want to let a dude with that kind of rap loose on the world—which made the pilot a sympathetic protagonist, if you were willing to overlook the illegal cargo. Or she might have been Japanese or Korean.

Perhaps they had meant to make a sequel of the movie but were thwarted when the only drive-in in America that actually showed *Island of the Doomed* burned down. It's not easy for an entire drive-in to burn down, including the screen, but this one did, and they claimed you could smell the marijuana all the way in Wisconsin. Anyhow, in the movie Satan tries to sweet-talk the Asian hottie into letting him out of the cave by promising to teach her how to pronounce the letter *L*. After struggling with her conscience—indicated by close-ups of her chewing her lip—she finally gives in and takes down the crosses, but he is so monstrously wicked that he teaches her *W* instead, and from then on she talks like Elmer Fudd. Which, of course, served her wight, and, looking back, I see now that the movie's strong moral message was that you shouldn't sneak your friends into the drive-in by stuffing them into the trunk of your car. Then they had an intermission, and you were supposed to put your pants back on and go to the refreshment stand.

When the movie resumed, the devil is having a rum punch and dreaming up creative and especially horrible ways to kill his visitors and immolate their souls, sort of like Jamaica during election season, and he comes up with a great plan. There is a sudden earthquake, and the island sinks. This movie was so bad that, until this moment, you did not know there was a problem with the earth, so apparently Lucifer diddled with the tectonic plates during intermission. Luckily the pilot repairs his plane, and he and his girlfriend escape in the nick of time. Another indication that this movie would not be an Oscar nominee was that the writer gave no indication where the pilot could possibly have bought spare parts. Aristotle, or one of those non-restaurant (although, come to think of it, you never know) Greek guys, called this kind of surprise resolution a *deus ex machina*, which is Greek for "soak the screen with more gasoline."

But the P of D has the last laugh because he secretly put a voodoo hex on the plane's instruments, and when the pilot thinks he's flying a thousand feet over the island's central mountain, in reality he's about to dive-bomb into his last sushi dinner. The plane crashes into the ocean with a fiery explosion, which made no sense to us even stoned, but we were not exactly Siskel and Ebert. Satan laughs diabolically and begins to swim to the mainland, where he will become a university professor and get tenure. As the movie ends, he's dog-paddling eerily into the fog and disappears. I have no doubt this is where the sequel would have begun, had the director not hanged himself.

The years passed. I forgot about that movie and, mercifully, the girl I saw it with—although I fulfilled my legal obligations to the penny. I went to college and got a degree in English literature, having lied to my parents, who thought I was going to law school. *Island of the Doomed* never entered my mind again. Until…

A few years ago I was researching a magazine article on Caribbean horseracing and was preparing to leave Antigua for Barbados. I had bought my ticket weeks earlier but, as always, called the day before the flight to try to get a good seat—which in this airline's case was anywhere not near the emergency exit door, because a warning sign above it says LOCK SECURELY BUT ONLY IF YOU REALLY, REALLY FEEL LIKE IT. I will not say the actual name of the airline because it is the West Indian national pastime to sue for slander, even though the West Indies is not a nation, which proves what hard-core fans of slander-suing they are. Here is a typical example of how it works.

SARAFINA BRANDYBOTTOM (in classified ad in local newspaper): I am hereby giving notice that on account of Reginal "Doopy Man" Newton of Sandy Grove Parish having told my best friend's mother's cousin Frederick "Brother Pinhead" Lawson, who drives the green minibus "Do It," that I have a skinny batty, I will be filing a lawsuit against said Reginal "Doopy Man" Newton for slander. Considering he is wanted in Barbados on charges of kidnapping, arson, and multiple murder, he should talk.

REGINAL "DOOPY MAN" NEWTON (in letter on editorial page of local newspaper): I'm going to sue SaraFina Brandybottom for slander for saying I'm wanted in Barbados on charges of kidnapping, arson, and multiple murder. These charges are outrageous and scurrilous and not entirely true.

SARAFINA BRANDYBOTTOM (in her reply in local newspaper): If Mr. Reginal "Doopy Man" Newton had only read my words more carefully, he would have seen that I said, "*Considering* that Reginal 'Doopy Man' Newton is wanted in Barbados on charges of kidnapping, arson, and multiple murder." I only said to "consider" it. I never said it was a fact. Obviously a person can consider it or not of his or her own free will, that is why we have democracy. But "considering" is not the same as saying it is so. Therefore I am going to sue Mr. Reginal "Doopy Man" Newton for slander, right after breakfast.

REGINAL "DOOPY MAN" NEWTON (newspaper): It apparently did not register on Miss Brandybottom that I said "I'm going to sue SaraFina Brandybottom," not that I'm going to sue any *particular* SaraFina Brandybottom. However, she accused me in a public forum of not reading "carefully," which is a slanderous offense, and I am therefore on my way right now to file a big lawsuit against her for slander. Here I go.

SARAFINA BRANDYBOTTOM (newspaper): Mr. Reginal "Doopy Man" Newton is saying that I am afraid of his threats, and anyone who knows me will testify that I am not afraid of him, and to say so is a libelous charge, and so now I am really, really, really going to sue him for slander. I mean it. That is me you see on the road heading to the courthouse.

And so on, with neither one ever quite getting around to popping for the $2.25 to record the paperwork, and even if they did, it would have been a waste of money, because they would have forgotten the original slander in the first place. But a good time would be had by all, and the next time Mr. Reginal "Doopy Man" Newton saw Miss Brandybottom waiting for a bus, he would honk, and she would wave back at him with her newspaper, and crowing roosters would still wake up tourists at three in

the morning, and Liberty Airlines—not its real name—
would continue to make otherwise law-abiding customers
wish to commit kidnapping, arson, and multiple murder.

Let me explain.

The young woman ticket agent on the phone at Liberty
said they had no record of my reservation. So right off the
bat I knew this was going to be one of those conversations
that came down to national sovereignty.

"I'm looking at the ticket right now," I explained, reading the particulars.

"No record," she explained in return.

"That's not possible."

"Hold on."

She put the phone down, and I could hear her talking
to her girlfriend Iris, evidently standing next to her at the
counter, about how Bob Marley died of "bad big toe," and
her own toe was throbbing, and did Iris think she was
going to die, too? And Iris said, "If you do, gal, can I have
your blue blouse and maybe that yellow pants but definitely not your shoes, because I sure as hell don't want to
get no bad-toe business."

Sometime later, during which my spinal disks fused, my
ticket agent, who refused to give me her name due to security reasons—perhaps I would hunt her down and infect
her other toe—picked up the phone again and told me,
"No reservation."

"I already paid for the ticket. I'm looking at the receipt.
Do you want the number again?"

"Hold on."

She put down the phone and asked Iris how you make
those hickeys that look like bougainvilleas, every time she
tries they come out like hubcaps, and Iris said that Bob

Marley had many girlfriends when he was married to Rita, and many of them claimed part of his estate, and my ticket agent said Iris better be careful, they would sue her for slander, and she asked if it was his left big toe or his right big toe, and Iris asked what difference it made, and my ticket agent said because if it was the same toe as hers, she was probably going to die.

I happened to be watching a cricket match on my hotel TV during this conversation, and as anyone who understands a wicky-twicket about that sport knows, a single game can last for several geological ages and only ends when one of the players dies from a glacier hitting him on the head. When the game I was watching began, the bowlers were young and robust, but by the time the agent from Liberty picked up the phone again, they were in a retirement home painting by numbers.

"No reservation."

"I absolutely have to get to Barbados tomorrow." My attitude was not threatening or belligerent in any way. On the contrary, as a veteran Caribbean traveler, I knew the best tone to take here was that of a pitiful, mewling whelp that had just been beaten with a rolled-up newspaper and was wailing for its miserable life.

"Well, my screen don't lie," she snapped. "That's slander." Her keyboard clickity-clacked. "I got a seat to Barbados next Thursday." Clackety-click. "Or I can get you to Guadeloupe tomorrow morning, and you would take Air Martinique back up to St. Martin. That's the best I can do. Yes or no?"

"That's the opposite direction," I whimpered. Anyhow, I had once taken an Air Martinique plane, and the flight attendant refused to let me use the toilet until I asked her in

French, and the Parisian next to me thought it was a riot, and he smelled like his flesh hadn't touched soap since the Louisiana Purchase. "I'll never get to Barbados on time."

"Hold on."

Iris told my ticket agent how some time ago she and her boyfriend, Bully Boy, "was going through problems, and for a time he wouldn't talk to me, nearly three weeks." Another guy she knew, Waddie, liked her a whole lot, but she didn't like him as much. He took her out a couple of times, and she made him buy her some clothes and jewelry. She only gave him sex once, and only because Bully Boy "going on like a pig." She really did not like Waddie, but she was just playing with him until Bully came around. Her family warned her, "if I lie down with dog I get flea." And then, what you think? One night Waddie drops her home and wants her to perform on him. "I told him no, so he get vex and lock all the car doors and tried to jump me." Bully, who was stalking her at the time, saw what was about to happen, took a rock and smashed the window. "So Waddie come out the car and beat Bully up bad, then mooma and daddy come out the house and he dread them up, too." Two police came, and because one of them was her family, "they rass him up on the ground, then handcuff him to the fence so I could spit on his face." Then her father went inside for a machete and "give Waddie a chop to his head." What she was trying to say, she told my agent, was that although her father was in jail and Bully Boy was in the hospital, the whole thing brought her family together. "Bully and me parents now real close. Mooma using Bully's car until he come out the coma." So everything worked out for the best. "Except now I meet a foreign man from Aruba who have a brain, and you know I am a gal attracted to big brain, so soon we was more than hi and hello." She asked my agent if "it wrong to flex with a foreign flavor while me boyfriend unconscious?"

My agent picked up the phone. "Still there?"

"Still here."

"Hold on."

She returned to Iris and huffed, "People always slapping a man on the back when he got two gal and saying they want to be just like him, but as soon as a woman do the same thing, she's a slut and get all kinda name." The agent believed they should change that, and she for one was going to change that because if she "want two man," she "going to have two man." One of her men, "Mr. High Roller," never asked for change and had a lot of style to him. He showed her nice things in life and in the bedroom. Her other fella, "Mr. Best Friend," gave her advice when she needed it and having problems. He was sweet and caring with a good sense of humor and didn't need to put a sock in his pants and pretend to be a gunslinger, "acting like he going on all night, then the moment you give him one nibble, he shoot up the whole Front Street." Mr. High Roller said women are not supposed to maintain two men, it's immoral. It's logical for a man to have more than one lover because they can see their mistress on Monday, girlfriend on Wednesday, and the wife gets the weekend. "But he say a gal got to cook, clean, and entice him, so how can she do all that and still have pep for another man?"

She picked the phone up—rather hostilely, if I wasn't mistaken. "What?!"

"I'm a toe doctor!"

Silence.

"World renowned toe doctor," I assured her. "From the United Nations Center on International Toe Epidemic Control. I have to get to Barbados to save a woman's foot pinky."

"Doctor! Doctor! *I* got what she got!"

"Don't kid."

"I mean it!"

"Highly unlikely."

"How you know?"

"I could tell at a glance, of course. Can you meet me at the gate in the morning?"

"I will be there!" Her keyboard clackety-clicked. "I have to bump someone."

"Do you happen to know if any French people are on the flight?"

Click-clack, clack-click. "I have a Mister Jean LeBoyer." She pronounced it *Gene*.

"Traveling alone?"

"With his wife."

"Bump him."

"Done."

"See you in the morning. *Au revoir.*"

Early the next day, she collared me at the check-in counter, and we went to the transfer lounge, she limping, and she sat down and took off her shoe. She wanted Iris there in case I gave her bad news and she fainted. Her toe looked fine. It was a handsome toe, in fact—polished the same powder blue as in the Antiguan flag, trimmed nice and neat and with nice proportions. It didn't look swollen in the least. I asked her to wiggle it, and she made a little figure eight in the air and pointed with it to the Carib Beer sign, and I could sense that she wanted me to feel it, wanted the reassurance of a doctor's touch. Instead, I asked her how it hurt, and she said, "Like the devil inside or something and want to get out but he can't." And then she did something I hadn't expected. She told me her name.

"Ramona."

That's what fear does to you. Ramona.

She wiggled her toe again and winced, and I thought about touching it to at least make her feel better but couldn't bring myself to do it.

"You not going to manipulate it?"

"It's just a little arthritis," I said. "Tell your regular doctor. He'll fix you up."

She frowned but thanked me anyhow and went limping away, and I had my reserved seat, and all in all I felt pretty victorious.

And then someone behind me gasped, and someone else whispered, "Lawd! Me mooma!" and I saw they were gaping at the lounge TV, and I glanced up and saw the first World Trade Center tower on fire.

And I suddenly remembered *Island of the Doomed*.

I had not thought of that drive-in movie in all those years, but now it sprang to my mind in Technicolor. I stared at that burning building and recalled how Lucifer had tricked the pilot's girlfriend into letting him loose on the world.

And then, weirdly, I imagined that smoking high-rise as Ramona's toe.

It occurred to me that there's a tiny devil barricaded in all of us. For the drive-in Satan it was a cave. For "Mr. High Roller," the front of his pants, and Ramona, frightened of dying like Bob Marley, her big toe. For me, he's in that part of my brain responsible for my not having been able to touch that perfectly nice foot.

The gate agent made his final call.

I glanced beyond the glass to the stairs leading to the ticket counter. There might still be time if I begged the gate agent for a few more minutes and sprinted, time to run back to the ticket counter and grab that toe and manipulate the hell out of it and tell Ramona the devil was gone and she was going to live a long, happy life.

The gate agent gathered his papers and was tap-blocking them on his countertop, while making one last perfunctory glance for stragglers. What happened on television didn't concern him. He had work to do. *Tap-tap*. His gaze met mine. I could have easily asked for a couple more minutes. But his eyes were two caves, so dark no light reflected in them. *Tap-tap*. Work.

I wanted to run back to Ramona but couldn't. I told myself that a true professional doesn't let himself get distracted by emotion. All right, I wasn't Woodward or Bernstein—but a deadline is still a deadline. So I got on the plane instead.

I was no match for Beelzebub.

So I would make the Barbados races after all, and my article would be written, and I'd see my name under the title, and I'd be as proud of myself as the director of *Island of the Doomed* must have been, and that's what I was thinking as Flight 19 roared into the trade wind, and by then, of course, it was too late to go back to comfort Ramona. We did a little bump-thump, and although usually I'm not a nervous flier, this time it struck me that I was going to die a fiery death, and I caught my breath and grabbed the armrest as if it were a big toe requiring big manipulation, and I could feel my own toes burning.

I squeezed my eyes and thought about those people hanging out the smoking windows and Ramona. And then I was overcome, consumed, with the belief that Flight 19 was never going to land, and my legs stiffened for a crash.

And then a hand clasped mine, and I was startled and opened my eyes and looked into very kind, calming ones. "It is all right," the woman next to me said, her English wrestling with her French. "*C'est bien.* Nothing to be afraid, *vous savez?*"

"*Je sais,*" I whispered, though I'm sure my American accent gave me away.

"We will arrive safely *ensemble,*" she said, taking my fist and putting it in her lap and caressing it with both of hers. "Together," she repeated in English, and Madam LeBoyer's was the most angelic face I have ever seen.